A Romantic Architect in Antebellum North Carolina:

The Works of Alexander Jackson Davis

EDWARD T. DAVIS

JOHN L. SANDERS

A joint publication of the Historic Preservation Foundation of North Carolina, Inc., and The State Capitol Foundation, Inc.

The Historic Preservation Foundation of North Carolina and The State Capitol Foundation dedicate this publication to John L. Sanders for his decades of devotion to the North Carolina State Capitol.

Front cover:
North Carolina State Capitol
Perspective drawn by A. J. Davis, ca. 1833
Metropolitan Museum of Art, Harris Brisbane Dick Fund

Back cover:
Montrose, Hillsborough, perspectives by A. J. Davis, 1851.
Courtesy of the Historic Preservation Foundation of North Carolina, Inc.

Exhibit curator:
Edward T. Davis

Publication project coordinators:
Rob Maddrey, Shannon Long, Lisa Pickett

Book design:
Pam Chastain Design, Durham

© 2000 Historic Preservation Foundation of North Carolina, Inc. All rights reserved.
ISBN Number: 0-9673037-1-0

Table of Contents

Sponsors	4
Foreword	7
". . . far fetched and dear bought . . . ": Alexander Jackson Davis in North Carolina	9
Alexander Jackson Davis and the North Carolina State Capitol	37
The Works by Alexander Jackson Davis in North Carolina	57
Bibliography	58
Acknowledgments	62

Sponsors

FOR SUPPORT OF THE EXHIBITION

Grand Patron

Richard H. Jenrette, New York

Patrons

Charles H. Babcock, Jr., Winston-Salem

Thomas S. Kenan III, Chapel Hill, *in memory of Sarah Graham Kenan*

North Carolina Estates, Research Triangle Park

J. N. Pease Associates, Charlotte

Katherine and Bev Webb, Edenton

Sponsors

Broyhill Family Foundation, Lenoir

Gwen P. and Charles A. Davis, Raleigh

Kathleen Bryan Edwards, Greensboro, *in memory of Kathleen Price Bryan*

The Frank Borden Hanes Charitable Lead Trust, Winston-Salem

J. Myrick Howard, Raleigh

AIA North Carolina

Mr. and Mrs. John P. Martin, Jr., Columbus

Mrs. Kenneth K. Millholland, Hickory, *in honor of Frances J. Moody and Myrick Howard*

Elizabeth Moore Ruffin, Raleigh

Monica C. Watson, Wilmington

Theron P. Watson, Forest City, *in memory of T. Max and Lillian B. Watson*

Emeritus Professors Charles M. and Shirley F. Weiss, Chapel Hill

Mr. and Mrs. Willliam Holt Williamson III, Charlotte

Donors

Gerald Allen, New York

Mr. and Mrs. David Paynter, Wilmington

Sarah Rhyne, Graham, *in memory of Myron A. Rhyne*

John L. Sanders, Chapel Hill

Virginia A. Stevens, Raleigh

Mary Arthur Stoudemire, Chapel Hill

Other Contributors

Sarah Bollinger, Winston-Salem, *in honor of Edward T. Davis*

William J. and Dorothy Gay Darr, High Point

Renee Gledhill-Earley, Raleigh

Thomas A. Gray, Winston-Salem

William H. Heins, Jr., Sanford

Roy H. Lawrence, Pinehurst, *in memory of Elizabeth S. Ives*

Dr. and Mrs. Robert E. Nolan, Winston-Salem

Dr. and Mrs. Ledyard E. Ross, Greenville

FOR SUPPORT OF THE PUBLICATION

Grand Patrons

The Michel Family Foundation, Greensboro

The State Capitol Foundation, Inc., Raleigh

Patrons

Richard H. Jenrette, New York

Amy and Damon Averill, Brevard (through the Community Foundation of Western North Carolina)

Sponsors

Gwendolyn Picklesimer Davis, Raleigh

Linda and Rufus Edmisten, Raleigh

J. Myrick Howard and Brinkley Sugg, Raleigh

Henry W. Lewis, Chapel Hill

Sylvia and Brent Nash, Tarboro

Virginia A. Stevens, Blowing Rock

Emeritus Professors Charles M. and Shirley F. Weiss, Chapel Hill

Donors

Zebulon D. Alley, Raleigh

Kaye Hollowell Barker, Edenton

Barbara Heilbroner Boney, Raleigh

Phillip C. Broughton and David L. Smith, Asheville

Mr. and Mrs. C. C. Cameron, Charlotte

Kay Bryan Edwards, Greensboro

Craufurd and Nancy Goodwin, Hillsborough

David R. Hayworth, High Point

Donald G. Mathews and Elizabeth F. Buford, Raleigh

Dr. and Mrs. John Lewis McCain, Wilson

Mr. and Mrs. John F. McNair III, Winston-Salem

Chief Justice Burley B. Mitchell, Jr., Raleigh

Joe and Langdon Oppermann, Winston-Salem

William S. and Virginia W. Powell, Chapel Hill

Mary Arthur Stoudemire, Chapel Hill

Sarah Denny Williamson, Raleigh

Other Contributors

Former State Representative George W. Breece, Fayetteville

Renee Gledhill-Earley, Raleigh

Foreword

A Romantic Architect in Antebellum North Carolina is not merely a compilation of images; rather, it is a parcel of North Carolina's history. It represents the combined efforts of several years' careful research and thoughtful writing on the part of its authors. It is also a tribute to North Carolina's leaders during the several decades prior to the Civil War who labored to take a sluggish and backward state and make it among the most progressive in the United States. Those leaders, whose names appear throughout this document, strove to create the finest system of public education in the nation, constructed the then-longest railroad in the world, and created institutions for the care of the blind, insane and deaf. They also commissioned one of the nation's preeminent architects, Alexander Jackson Davis, for the design of their public and private edifices.

Further, this publication also honors the many North Carolinians who for generations have worked to preserve the architectural legacy of A. J. Davis in North Carolina — especially John Sanders.

The impetus for *A Romantic Architect in Antebellum North Carolina* is a traveling exhibition about Alexander Jackson Davis. Collaboratively sponsored by Preservation North Carolina and the Gallery of Art & Design at North Carolina State University, the exhibition was originally made possible by the generosity of more than forty private donors. The kind support of additional donors has enabled Preservation North Carolina and The State Capitol Foundation to complete this publication. We are most grateful to all.

It is with great pleasure that we invite you to explore the ideas and aspirations of these leaders and to delight in the buildings that Alexander Jackson Davis created and proposed for the state. We hope you will attain a new and deeper appreciation for this remarkable period in North Carolina's history.

J. Myrick Howard
Executive Director, Preservation North Carolina

Rufus L. Edmisten
President, The State Capitol Foundation, Inc.

Charlotte V. Brown
Director, North Carolina State University Gallery of Art & Design

Beverly Ayscue
Coordinator, North Carolina Architectural Heritage Exhibitions

North Carolina State Capitol, Raleigh, Rotunda, photograph by Tim Buchman, 2000

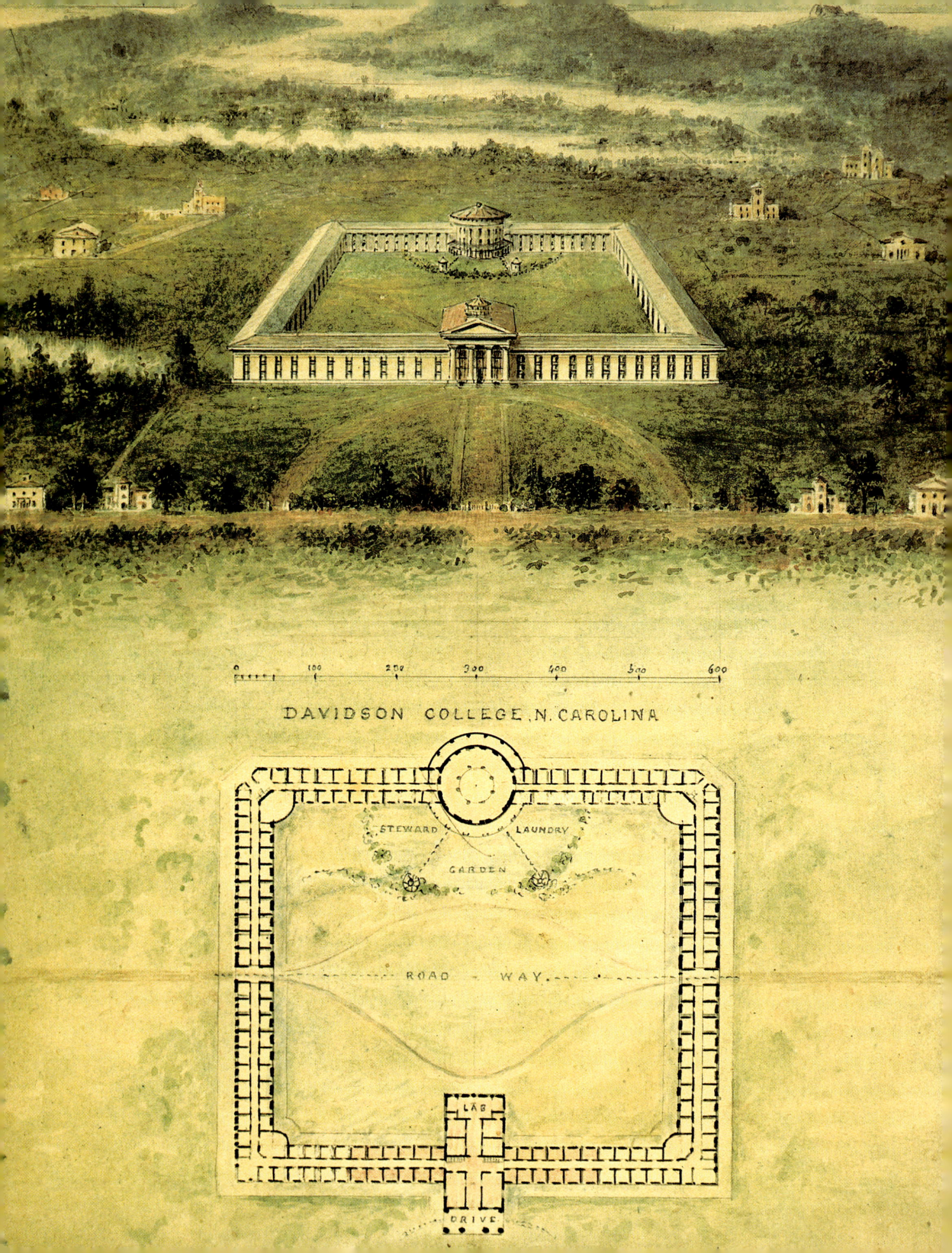

"... far fetched and dear bought ...":
Alexander Jackson Davis in North Carolina

EDWARD T. DAVIS

> *Seeing a very decent looking stranger in the street the other day, I inquired who he was, and was informed he was an Architect, who had come all the way from the City of New York, to submit plans and superintend the erection of two buildings at the University of North Carolina. ... The trustees of the University are public agents and the people at large have an interest in all they do, and a right to criticize their acts. I had hoped that they were above the passion for the "far fetched and dear bought ..."*[1]

Prior to the advent of the railroad and the sweeping economic, social and political changes enabled by the state constitutional reforms of 1835, North Carolina was an isolated, rural state, primarily populated by self-sustaining farmers. The state was so underdeveloped and apathetic that it was termed "the Rip Van Winkle State," "the Ireland of America" and the "second Nazareth."

> A legislative committee reported in 1830 that the state was without foreign commerce, for want of seaports, or a staple; without internal communication by rivers, roads, or canals; without a cash market for any article of agricultural produce; without manufactures; in short without any object to which native industry and active enterprise could be directed.[2]

State government, dominated by wealthy landowners from the eastern counties, was controlled by a one-party system. These elected state officials held that state government should tax little and spend less. Internal improvements were seen as matters of individual, private concern. The economy of the state stagnated.

While the overwhelming majority of the population lived simply in small log structures, persons in some areas of the state accumulated significant wealth and built stylish plantation houses and townhouses. These buildings, however, were largely constructed by local artisans and were based on tradition-

Fig. 1. Davidson College, Davidson, drawing by A. J. Davis. From the Alexander Jackson Davis Archives, Avery Architectural and Fine Arts Library, Columbia University in the City of New York, 1955.001.00250.

Fig. 2. Presbyterian Church in Fayetteville, after a drawing by Amanda (?) Barge, 1832.

al plan-forms embellished with local interpretations of details derived from architectural pattern books.

Architect-designed buildings had been constructed before Alexander Jackson Davis (1803-1892) began producing designs for North Carolina clients, the most noteworthy of these being the works of English-born architects John Hawks and William Nichols. These were rare. Even the wealthiest clients called upon local builders and artisans to provide designs for both private and public buildings. In stark contrast to their peers in the neighboring states to the north and south, many prosperous landholders often chose to live in simple structures, shunning outward signs of affluence.

In 1835, the Whig Party was consolidated by an alliance of the increasingly populous and disgruntled western Piedmont counties and the old Sound regions of the state. In firm alliance against the older, wealthier counties of the east, ambitious legislators passed a series of constitutional reforms which inaugurated 25 years of remarkable developments.

Between the years 1835 and 1860, state government established institutions for the blind, the deaf and the mentally ill, constructed one of the nation's most magnificent state capitol buildings, provided major financial support for one of the finest statewide systems of public schools in the nation prior to the Civil War, and gave financial backing for the longest railroad constructed in the world at that time. Because of increased capital resulting from these extensive improvements, many private enterprises were established, agricultural conditions were greatly improved and factories and textile mills—institutions which would later transform the state's economy—were constructed.

Fig.3 A. J. Davis Business Card. From the Alexander Jackson Davis Archives, Avery Architectural and Fine Arts Library, Columbia University in the City of New York, 1940.001.00151.

Progressive state leaders William Gaston of New Bern, Governor David L. Swain, the Reverend Joseph Caldwell, and Governor John Motley Morehead seized every opportunity to advance the state on all fronts. Not satisfied with simply improving prevailing conditions, they sought the most ambitious economic, social, political, and aesthetic ideals attainable. The new and growing

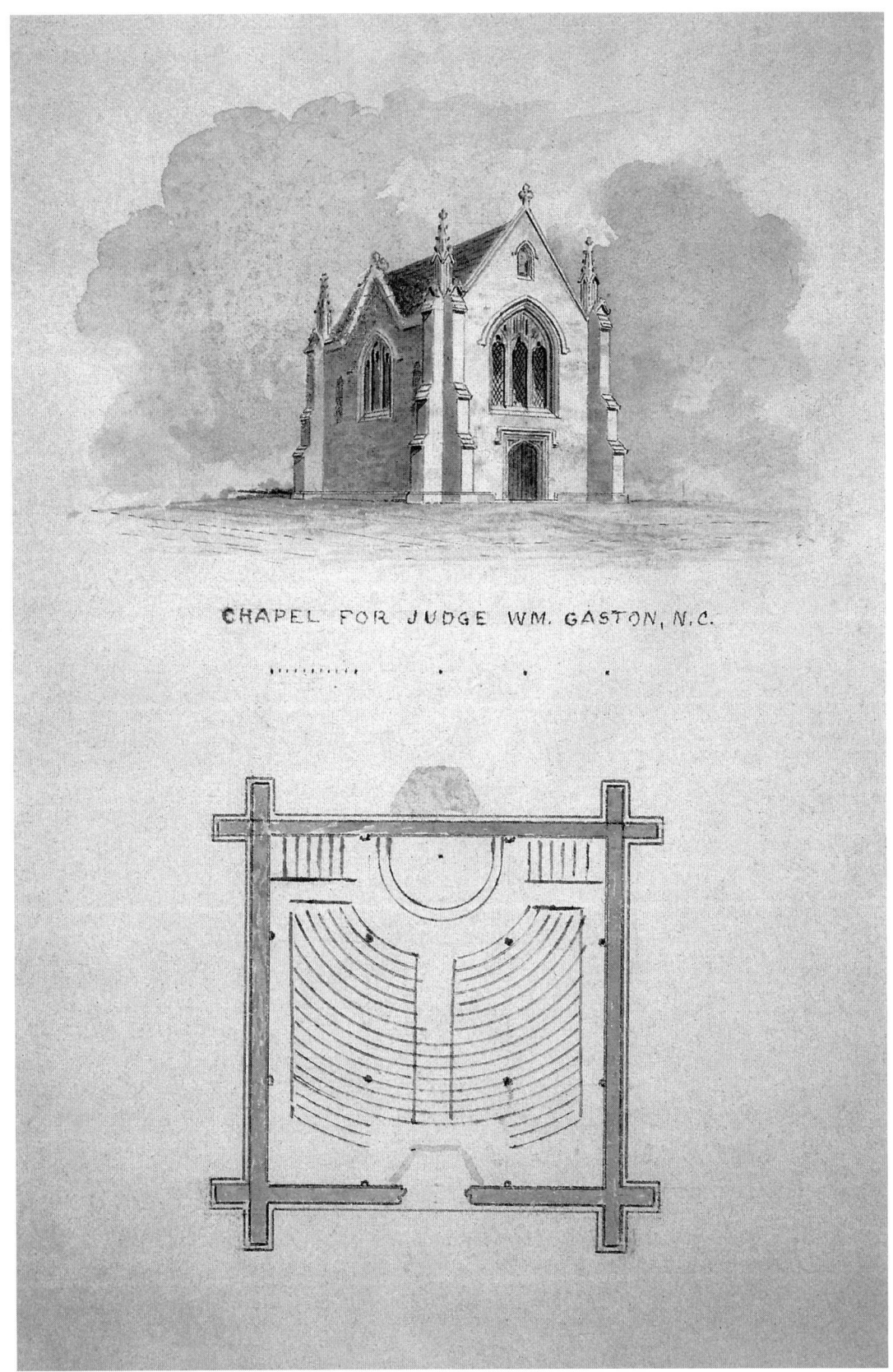

Fig. 4. Chapel for Judge William Gaston, New Bern, drawing by A. J. Davis. From the Alexander Jackson Davis Archives, Avery Architectural and Fine Arts Library, Columbia University in the City of New York, 1955.0001.00386.

Fig. 5. Premium Drawing for the U.S. Customs House, New York, drawing by A.J. Davis, 1833. M. & M. Karolik Collection of American Watercolors and Drawings, 1800-19875. Courtesy, Museum of Fine Arts, Boston, 50.3851.

institutions established for these purposes required modern buildings. And while other nationally prominent architects were called upon to design buildings in North Carolina, the state's leaders most frequently looked to one of the young nation's foremost tastemakers—Alexander Jackson Davis.

Fig. 6. Sarcophagus for Judge William Gaston, Cedar Grove Cemetery, New Bern, photograph by Tim Buchman, from *Sticks and Stones* by M. Ruth Little, 1998.

Davis was born in New York City on July 24, 1803. His father, Cornelius, was a bookseller and publisher of religious tracts. At age 15, Davis was sent to Alexandria, then in the District of Columbia, to apprentice with his half-brother Samuel, who was the editor of the *Alexandria Gazette*. While Davis learned typesetting under his brother's tutelage, he also spent time sketching the reconstruction of nearby Washington (partially destroyed by the War of 1812), explored literature and, importantly, took great interest in drama and the theater.

Davis returned to New York at age 20, where he worked as a draftsman and an architectural illustrator, and spent his spare time studying the architectural

Fig. 7. Plan for the University of North Carolina, Chapel Hill, drawing by A. J. Davis, 1856. Metropolitan Museum of Art, Harris Brisbane Dick Fund, 24.66.1406(30).

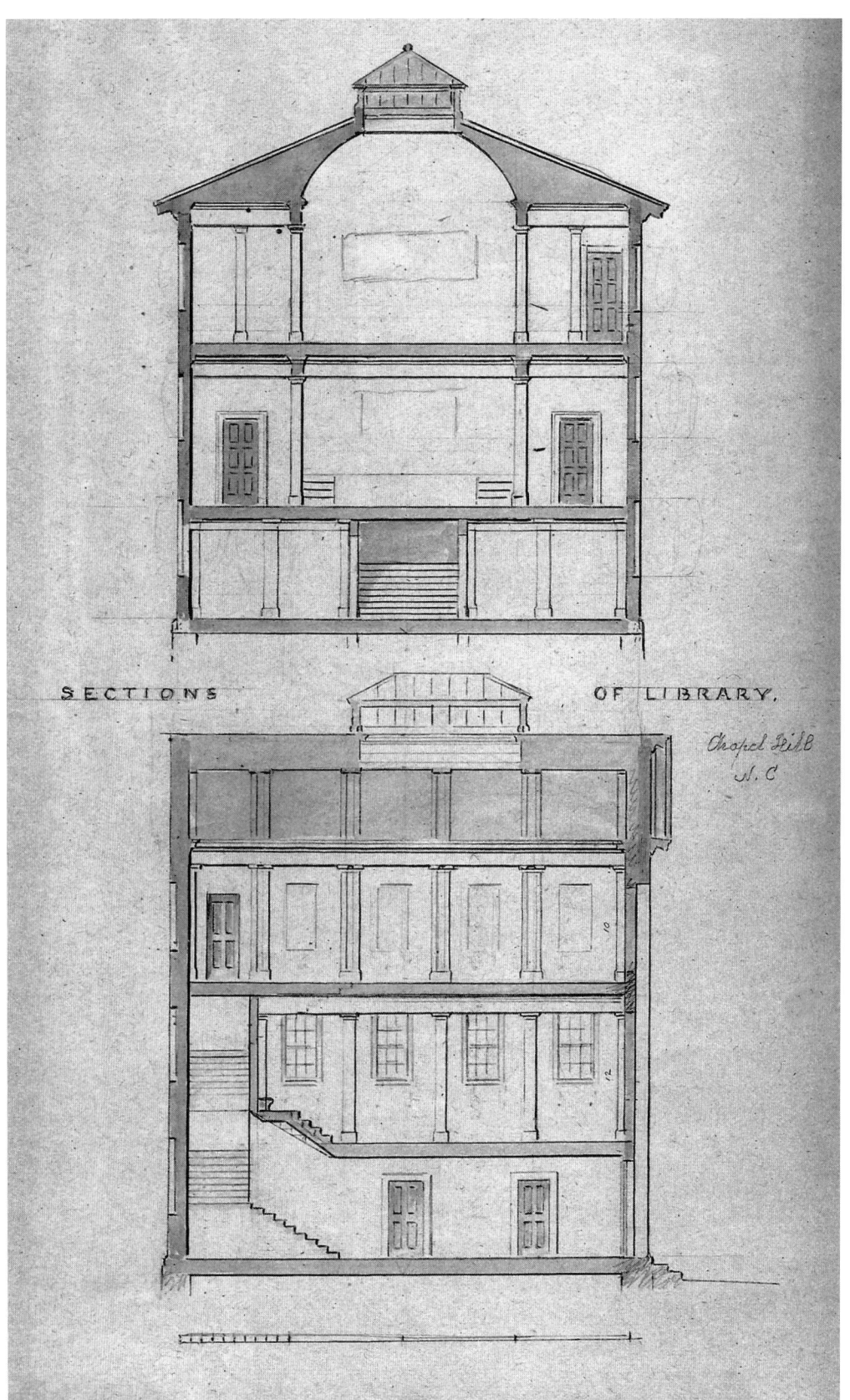

Fig. 8. Old East Building, University of North Carolina, Chapel Hill, drawing by A. J. Davis, 1844. Metropolitan Museum of Art, Harris Brisbane Dick Fund, 24.66.1406.

Fig. 9. Old East Building, University of North Carolina, Chapel Hill, photographer unknown, late 19th-century photograph. North Carolina Collection, University of North Carolina Library at Chapel Hill.

library of his future partner, Ithiel Town. Davis records in his journal

> 1828, March 15. First study of Stuart's Athens, from which I date Professional Practice . . . borrowed from Town.[3]

Davis was referring to Ithiel Town's copy of Stuart and Revett's *The Antiquities of Athens*. While Davis, who coined himself "Architectural Composer" (fig. 3.), had a preoccupation and passion for the Greek Revival throughout his adult life, he was part of a larger, international artistic movement known as "Romanticism."

Romanticism was actually a group of movements which began by incorporating both the study of Neoclassicism, which focused on renewal of the arts, and fresh reinterpretations of Roman, Egyptian, and Etruscan art and architecture. As the movements grew, more divergent and varied possibilities began to emerge. Architectural historian Charles Brownell, in discussing this era in American architecture has written,

> In architecture, many kinds of non-Classical inspiration became acceptable. New principles fit for a while into the old culture but then diverged from Classical values, as in the case of the Picturesque Movement. The devotees of the Picturesque learned to

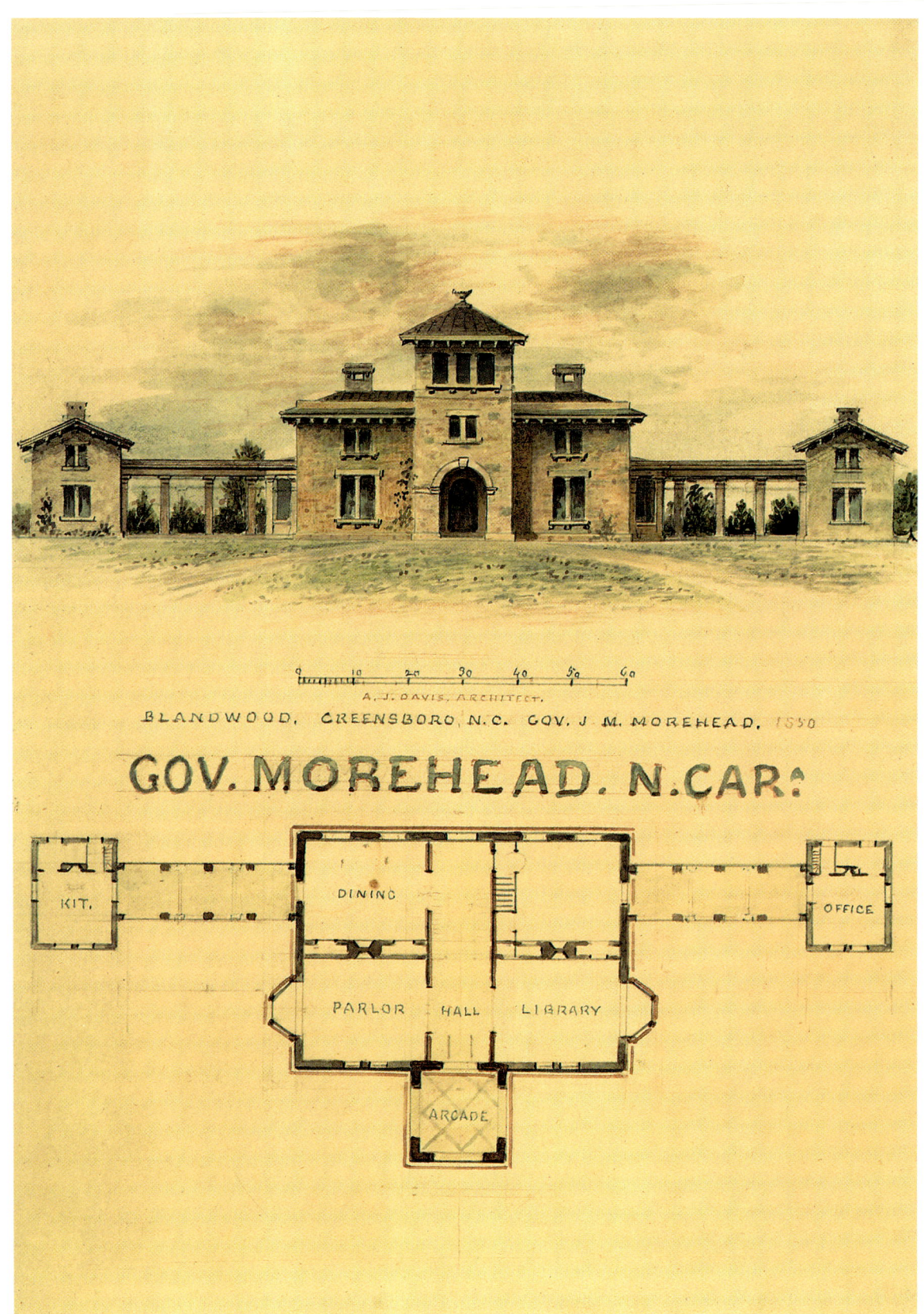

Fig. 10. Blandwood, Greensboro, drawing by A. J. Davis, 1844. Metropolitan Museum of Art, Harris Brisbane Dick Fund, 24.66.1405(119).

enjoy natural scenery as a shifting series of well-composed 'pictures' to walk through. They extended this appreciation to buildings, which they saw, not as embodiments of unchanging Classical principles, but as 'architectural scenery.'[4]

Davis, with his interest in theatrics, coupled with his unparalleled drafting skills, excelled at the creation of architecture as "architectural scenery." Ithiel Town, who made Davis his partner in 1829 — a partnership which would last six years and be revived briefly in 1842-1843, was an experienced engineer, proponent of the Greek Revival, and an innovative designer of lattice trusses, but he was no illustrator. Their partnership was entirely complementary. It produced some of the most remarkable buildings in America: the New York Custom House (fig. 5.), hospitals, banks, the Capitols of Indiana and North Carolina, town halls, churches, and city and country houses.

Fig. 11. Blandwood, Interior. Photograph courtesy of Preservation Greensboro, Inc.

Following his partnership with Town and a brief association with Russell Warren in 1835, Davis kept his own office alone. And for more than a decade, beginning in 1839, his association with American landscape architect, tastemaker and author Andrew Jackson Downing popularized Davis's designs and brought him both fame and an impressive list of commissions. His work extended from Maine to North Carolina and west to Ohio and Michigan, and he earned a distinguished place in the history of American architecture.

Ithiel Town had already established himself in North Carolina as a designer of wooden truss bridges when he and the younger architect joined together to form Town and Davis. The firm's first

Fig. 12. Dr. David Weir House, Greensboro, drawing by A. J. Davis, 1844. Metropolitan Museum of Art, Harris Brisbane Dick Fund, 24.66.1020.

Fig. 13. William J. Rotch House, New Bedford, Massachusetts, drawing by A. J. Davis, 1845. Metropolitan Museum of Art, Harris Brisbane Dick Fund, 24.66.20.

commission in the state was to rebuild the Presbyterian church in Fayetteville, which had burned in a fire in 1831 that had also destroyed much of the town.

Robert Donaldson, who was among Davis's most influential and important patrons, was a native of Fayetteville and a devout Presbyterian. As a courtesy to Donaldson, Town and Davis provided plans for the new church at no charge. Davis's daybook records that he presented a design for the new structure in 1831. The only period sketch of the church, however, reveals a simple meetinghouse devoid of any stylish architectural embellishments (fig. 2). Ithiel Town's roof truss system is extant, and it may be possible that simplifications to Davis's design were made by a local contractor, or perhaps the elevations provided by Davis were never utilized.[5]

In 1831, the North Carolina State House burned and a commission was established to seek its replacement. Town and Davis's initial proposal, which incorporated many of the features of Town's earlier design for the Connecticut State Capitol (1827) and the firm's recent Indiana State Capitol (1831-35), was rejected in favor of a design presented by William Nichols, Sr., and his son William, Jr. William Nichols, Sr., was the architect who had remodeled the earlier North Carolina State House, and his accepted design largely followed the form of the older building. But for reasons unknown, the commissioners dismissed the Nicholses after construction began, and appointed Town and Davis as architects of the Capitol in 1833. The firm's resulting building is the most important civic structure ever built in North Carolina. Because Town and Davis were forced to use a cruciform plan, as opposed to their earlier proposals modeled on temple-form buildings that they had designed previously, the Capitol stands as one of the firm's most innovative and unusual Greek Revival buildings.

In June 1834, Davis provided several sketches for a Roman Catholic chapel to be constructed in New Bern (fig. 4). The designs were presented to North Carolina's leading Roman Catholic, William

Gaston. Gaston had served in the state legislature, the Congress, was a judge of the North Carolina Supreme Court and was counselor to many famous persons throughout the United States. He was also the father-in-law of Robert Donaldson. In 1840, Davis made additional plans for a larger church, but it was never built. Roman Catholicism was not a populous denomination in nineteenth-century North Carolina, and funds were not available for so elaborate a structure. When William Gaston died in 1844, Davis donated a design for Gaston's sarcophagus to Susan Gaston Donaldson as a token of his admiration. Executed by Launitz in Italian marble, it is prominently situated in the Cedar Grove Cemetery at New Bern (fig. 6).

In 1843, Davis was hired to provide designs for the expansion of the University in Chapel Hill. The University of North Carolina had been chartered in 1789 and in 1795 it was the first state university to open its doors.

During the first 40 years of its existence, the development of the campus was piecemeal. The initial buildings were simple brick structures. Former Governor David L. Swain was selected president of the university in 1836. Swain realized that the village of Chapel Hill and the University were interdependent and took great interest in the improvement and development of both. He quickly appointed an experienced mechanic and builder as superintendent of university buildings and created the position of bursar for the oversight and improvement of the ornamental grounds adjacent to the small campus, as well as the extensive university lands.

The school had outgrown the five unadorned brick buildings constructed between

Fig. 14. Presbyterian Church, Chapel Hill, drawing by A. J. Davis, 1847. Metropolitan Museum of Art, Harris Brisbane Dick Fund, 24.66.1233.

Fig. 15. St. Paul's Covent Garden, London, England, engraving, artist unknown. Lent anonymously.

Fig. 16. Presbyterian Church, Chapel Hill, photographer unknown, 19th-century photograph. North Carolina Collection, University of North Carolina Library at Chapel Hill.

1793 and 1843, and Swain contacted university alumnus Robert Donaldson for advice on selecting an appropriate architect. Donaldson enthusiastically endorsed his old friend:

> . . . He is the readiest & most skillful Draughtman (sic) that I know. In fact, the Danger is, when he mounts the Pegasus of Design . . . there might be too much temptation held out by his fertile inventions & suggestions.[6]

This was not Davis's first contact with the University. He had previously provided a plan for the Philanthropic Society building in 1832, and in 1835 presented a design for a monument to Joseph Caldwell, former president of the University of North Carolina. However, neither project had been realized due to lack of funds. President Swain was familiar with the work of Town and Davis, having served as governor during the design and early construction phases of the magnificent Capitol building in Raleigh. It was logical for Swain to confer with Donaldson, the latter having established himself as a gentleman of supremely good taste.

Davis was engaged in 1843, serving as the primary planner, architect and landscape architect for the university for the next sixteen years. During this period the full range of his prolific skills would well-serve the university, the state and private clients, and North Carolina became an unlikely but fertile proving ground for the Picturesque movement in mid-nineteenth-century America.

Davis reached Chapel Hill on January 31, 1844. He met with the faculty on February 2, began plans for enlarging East and West buildings, and proposed improvements to the Chapel and the South Building. He presented these specific proposals, as well as the first of many masterplans locating botanical gardens, walks, gates, memorial statuary and a campanile.

For East and West buildings, Davis designed identical three-story additions for the north facade of each building. The additions provided additional dormitory spaces, "odeons" or debating halls for the Philanthropic and Dialectic societies (the university's debating clubs) on the second level, and libraries and reading rooms illuminated by monitors located above the barrel vaults on the third level (fig. 8).

Four colossal antapilasters define the exterior facade, producing the effect of a colonnade without the expense and construction difficulties inherent in the construction of freestanding columns. The window openings on this elevation are located in the central recessed shaft, between the antapilasters, and occupy a single plane. This device Davis immodestly called "Davisean windows." Davis explained the arrangement to President Swain:

> By paneling the whole space between the pilasters of the N. front we may pierce any of the panels for lights. Besides we would give a commonplace character even at the hazard of a contrast with the sides of the building. The trees will shut out the two contrasting faces. . . . And if they should not, it will be better (in my mind) that the buildings have one redeeming characteristic feature—one good eye, altho' that be Cyclopean in its character.[7]

A new bracketed cornice marries the new building and the old. The buildings were initially planned to be stuccoed, scored and painted to resemble stone. Budget restrictions, however, only per-

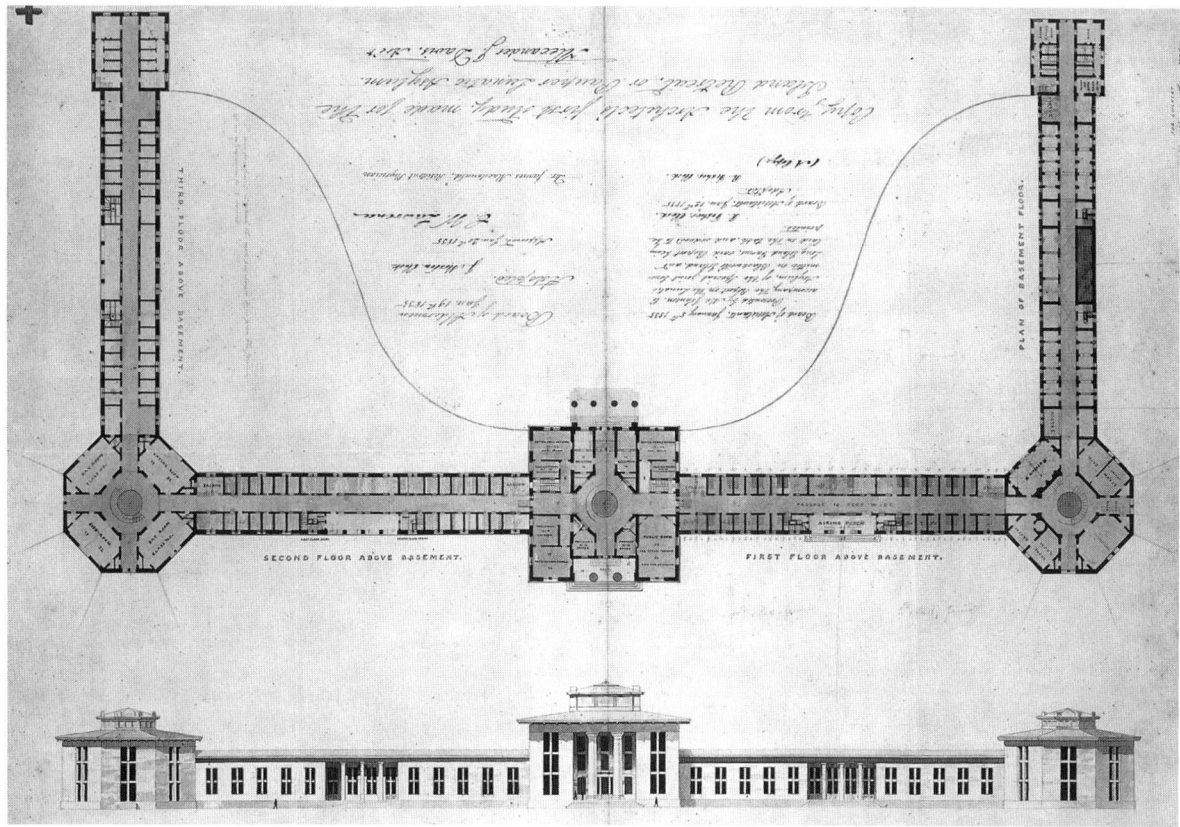

Fig. 17. Pauper Lunatic Asylum, Blackwell's Island, New York, New York, drawing by A. J. Davis, 1834. Metropolitan Museum of Art, Harris Brisbane Dick Fund, 24.66.452.

mitted a tinted wash (fig. 9). Free black artisan Thomas Day of Milton was the joiner for the interior woodwork and furnishings for these two additions.

The use of antapilasters in boldly defining exterior elevations was a passion which would occupy Davis throughout his career. While Davis usually reserved their application for commercial or institutional structures, as early as 1831 he was also experimenting with their use on a large residential apartment building in New York City.

The additions to East and West buildings accomplished two important tasks. As self-conscious, high-style spaces, both the

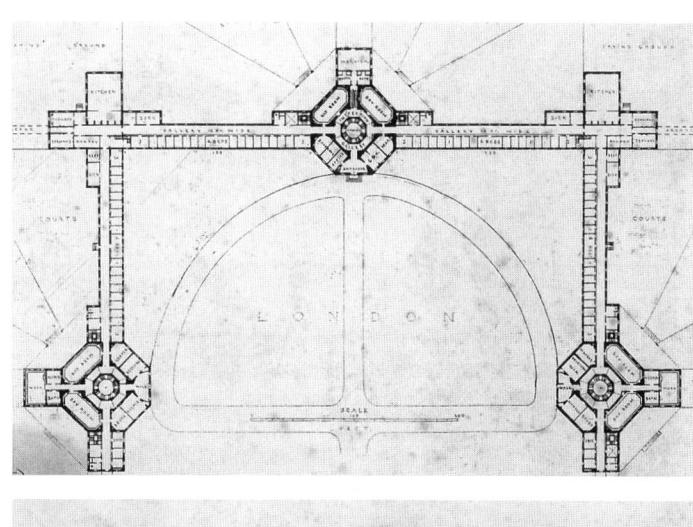

Fig. 18. Middlesex Hospital, London, England, ca. 1830. Metropolitan Museum of Art, Harris Brisbane Dick Fund, 24.66.1403.

A Romantic Architect in Antebellum North Carolina: The Works of Alexander Jackson Davis   21

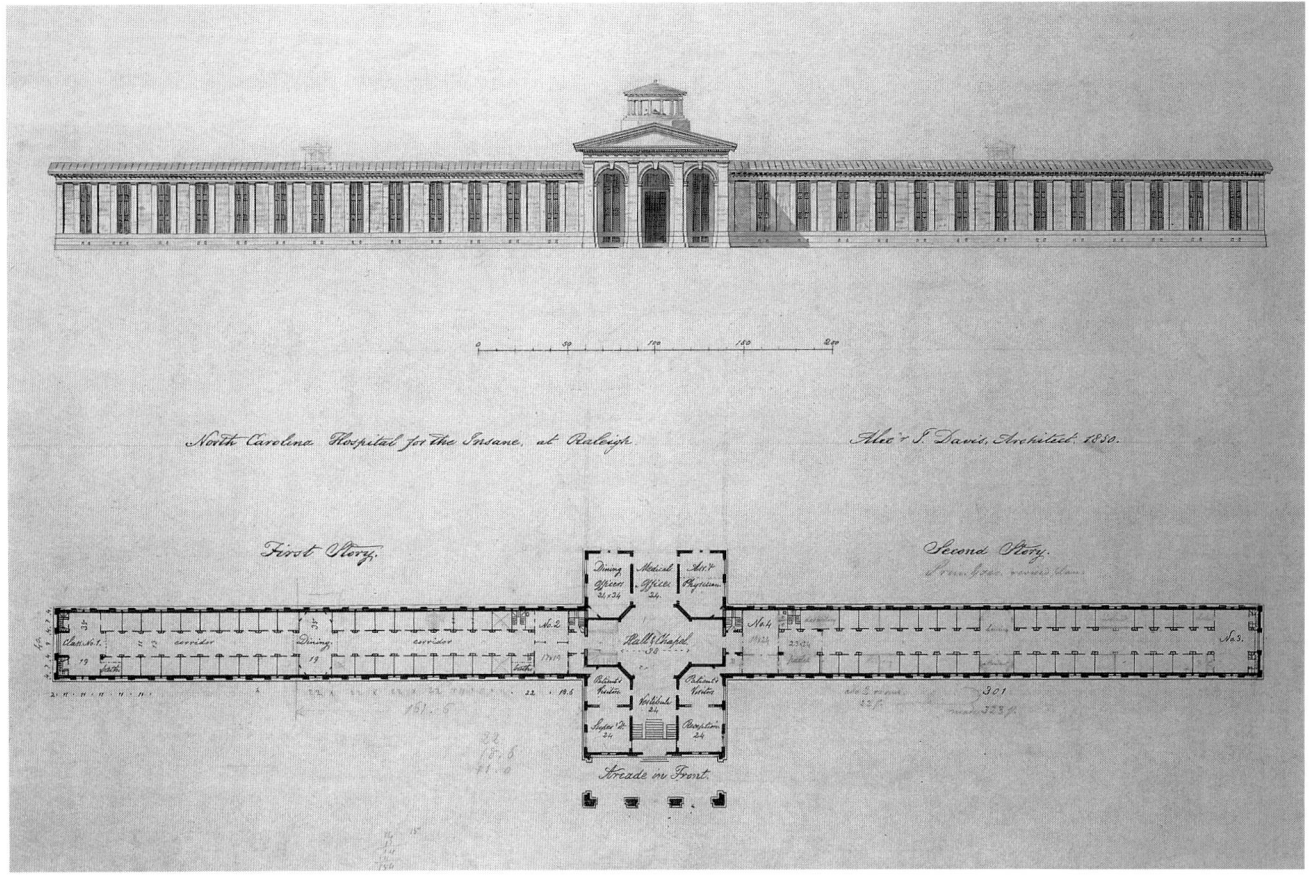

Fig. 19. North Carolina Hospital for the Insane (Dorothea Dix Hospital), Raleigh, drawing by A. J. Davis, 1850. Metropolitan Museum of Art, Harris Brisbane Dick Fund, 24.66.431.

odeons and libraries provided a lesson in aesthetics for the students. Secondly, the north elevations addressed the village of Chapel Hill as an *orderly*, if august, modern campus.

Davis concluded his meetings with President Swain and the university trustees in early February of 1844. Governor John Motley Morehead requested Davis to accompany him to Blandwood, his home in Greensboro, and design "additions" to the late eighteenth-century house which he had purchased from his father-in-law several years earlier. Davis stayed in Greensboro with the governor for three days and returned to Raleigh for two weeks to complete the drawings. The resulting building, as one of the early prototypes for the American Italianate style, is of national significance.[8]

Governor Morehead is counted among North Carolina's most progressive leaders. Educated by the famous Presbyterian minister the Reverend David Caldwell, he entered the University of North Carolina with advanced standing at age 19. He was a college mate of Robert Donaldson. He later read law with the visionary attorney and statesman Archibald DeBow Murphey in Hillsborough, and became a state senator, governor, textile industry leader and advocate and later president of the North Carolina Railroad. He was a man of enormous vision, often called "the father of modern North Carolina." It is therefore logical that he would select Davis to design additions to his home and that he would have the conviction to construct them.

Fig. 20. North Carolina Hospital for the Insane (Dorothea Dix Hospital), Raleigh. Photograph of exterior courtesy North Carolina Division of Archives and History.

Davis's additions largely envelop the original dwelling. Indeed, Davis's later sketch of Blandwood (fig. 10) could easily be interpreted as a new, freestanding, structure. No graphic reference in this sketch is made to the older building located immediately behind the central block of the "additions." Davis believed that house and landscape should be complementary. The wilder the landscape, the more irregular the house design. Jane Davies, the principal scholar of the life and works of Davis, explains that Davis believed

> a country house should be related to its setting in a unity of landscape and architecture. A country house, to harmonize with the irregularities of nature should not be a plain rigid box, but should have irregularities.[9]

Blandwood was essentially an urban house, located on the edge of the small city (figs. 10 and 11). The house appears, therefore, symmetrical, as appropriate to its location. Davis charged Governor Morehead $100.00 for the complete set of plans.[10]

While in Greensboro, Davis was introduced to a friend of Morehead's, Dr. David Weir. Dr. Weir commissioned Davis to design a house for him (fig. 12). Davis's design, an elegant cruciform plan,

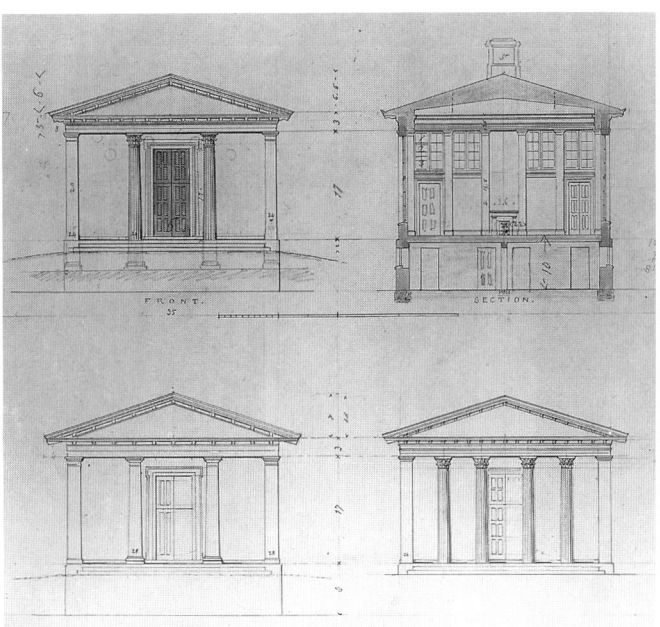

Fig. 21. Smith Hall Studies, University of North Carolina, Chapel Hill, drawing by A. J. Davis, 1850. Metropolitan Museum of Art, Harris Brisbane Dick Fund, 24.66.1801.

Fig. 22. "Corn Order" from The Capitol, Washington, District of Columbia, designed by Benjamin Henry Latrobe, 1809, drawing by A. J. Davis, ca. 1850. Metropolitan Museum of Art, Harris Brisbane Dick Fund, 24.656.1407[9].

illustrates the architect's tendency to modify designs supplied for other clients. The bold elevations, dominated by a central gable, are variations of the 1843 Delamater House in Rhinebeck, New York, in 1843 and the Rotch House (fig. 13) in New Bedford, Massachusetts, designed a year after the Weir commission.

Robert and James Donaldson hired Davis to design a Presbyterian church for Chapel Hill in 1847. The president and a majority of the faculty were Presbyterians. Chapel services, while ecumenical (though Protestant), were largely led by members of this denomination. The impetus for this Presbyterian structure may well have been the construction of the Chapel of the Cross, a small, elegant Gothic Revival church designed by Thomas U. Walter for Chapel Hill Episcopalians in 1842.

Donaldson and President Swain initially requested a Gothic building, but Davis advised that the cost of a Gothic tower alone would be prohibitive. Davis suggested an economical style he termed "Vitruvian Tuscan." The design he produced (fig. 14), a bracketed Tuscan temple, was based on the first English Protestant church built after the Reformation, St. Paul's Covent Garden by architect Inigo Jones in 1631 (figs. 15 and 16). In true Picturesque fashion, Davis advised the mason to paint the church "lilac grey." This color had been recommended by Andrew Jackson Downing (1814-1852) in his 1842 publication *Cottage Residences*.[11]

In 1842, and again in 1846, governors John Motley Morehead and William A. Graham recommended a state-supported facility for the care of the mentally ill. The General Assembly took no action on the matter until 1848, when the New England reformer Dorothea L. Dix evaluated the treatment of the insane during a three-month survey of conditions in North Carolina. Miss Dix ingeniously solicited the support of Cumberland County Democratic leader James C. Dobbin, whose wife she had visited and greatly comforted during a long and debilitating illness. On her deathbed Mrs. Dobbin requested that her husband secure funding for a state lunatic hospital. In the Davis-designed House of Commons in the state Capitol, Dobbin delivered an eloquent and emotional plea to the

General Assembly to establish a state lunatic asylum on the grounds of "charitable necessity." The measure passed. Former Governor Morehead, "Chairman of the Lunatic Committee," awarded this prestigious commission to Davis in December of 1849. Davis's journals record that he had met with Morehead two months previously in New York to review Davis's design for the Pauper Lunatic Asylum located at Blackwell's Island, New York (fig. 17). True to the mission of the progressive North Carolina reformers, Morehead requested that the facility, to be located just outside Raleigh, be "the best in the nation."[12]

Both the Pauper Lunatic Asylum and the North Carolina hospital were based on the much publicized Middlesex Lunatic Hospital located in London (fig. 18). Davis's own interpretation of this Middlesex project was a symmetrical composition relieved by antapilasters and Davisean windows and dominated by a central monumental three-story bracketed block with a pediment supported by Tuscan piers. The piers were married by soaring arches and the building was crowned with a circular belvedere. It later served as a model for other large, institutional complexes housed under one roof. The massive hospital, set on a hill just outside of Raleigh, was designed to be seen from a great distance. The scale of the Tuscan piers, the fenestration, antapilasters and belvedere reflect Davis's skill in manipulating proportion. It is equal in quality and scale to any of his important civic designs, and Davis himself called it "a great work" (figs. 19 and 20).

Its design embodied the philosophy of the leading asylum planners in the nation. Each patient's room had its own window. There were grounds for cultivation, gaslights, indoor plumbing and an advanced heating and ventilation system. At the time of its completion, it was both the largest and the most modern building in the state. The lunatic asylum, later appropriately named "Dorothea Dix Hospital," drew national attention as one of the most progressive institutions for the insane in the nation.

While completing the plans for the lunatic asylum, Davis began to prepare preliminary drawings for a building to house the unlikely combination of library and ballroom for the university in Chapel Hill. The resulting building, originally Smith Hall (subsequently known as Alumni Hall and now known as Playmakers Theater) is one of Davis's most imaginative academic buildings. As early as 1846, disgruntled University students at Chapel Hill had called for the construction of a ballroom.[13] When some university-owned properties were sold in 1847, the students demanded that the proceeds be directed towards the construction of a spacious new building to serve as a ballroom and an assembly room for commencement exercises. To these programmatic requirements were added those of a library by the trustees! The building was sited to complete the symmetrical composition of the principal structures of the university (fig. 7).

For over a year, Davis sent President Swain a series of studies. This was to be his first entirely new structure designed for the campus, and he meticulously studied many stylistic alternatives, including Tuscan, Doric, Corinthian

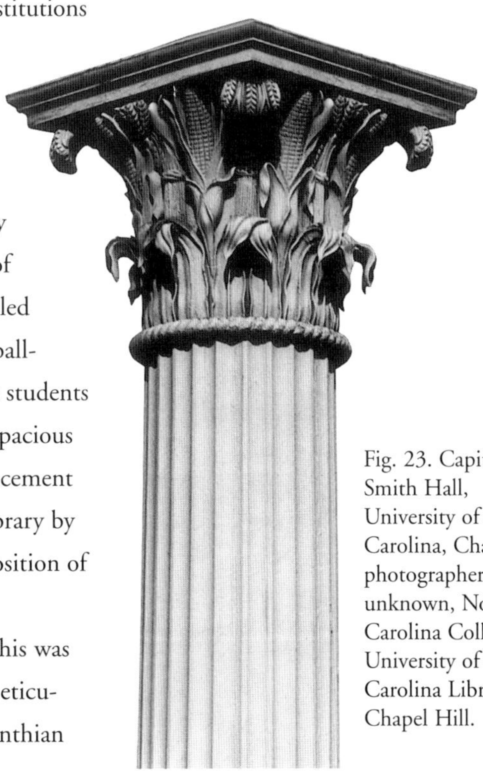

Fig. 23. Capital, Smith Hall, University of North Carolina, Chapel Hill, photographer unknown, North Carolina Collection, University of North Carolina Library at Chapel Hill.

A Romantic Architect in Antebellum North Carolina: The Works of Alexander Jackson Davis

and one which Davis called "Elevation Hexastyle" (fig. 21). The final design incorporated four freestanding Corinthian columns, which Davis believed followed an example from Athens. The Corinthian capitals were not composed of acanthus leaves, but of American corn and wheat—a device which Davis had seen in B. Henry Latrobe's work for the United States Capitol (fig. 22).[14] The elegant capitals for Chapel Hill (fig. 23), carved by Crane and Smith in New York, are greatly improved versions of Latrobe's original "American order." The exterior of the brick building was stuccoed, scored and painted gray to simulate granite (fig. 24).

The interior of the building illustrates the architect's genius. The walls were lined with delicately detailed Doric pilasters. The spaces between the pilasters housed shelves for books. At times of assemblies, balls, and commencements, muslin curtains, or blinds, could be rolled down over the books and secured to the baseboards. The blinds were appropriately painted with flowers which lent a festive appearance to an otherwise somber interior (fig. 25). This ingenious interior was largely destroyed when the building was converted into a theater in 1925.

Smith Hall, in no small measure, represents Davis's architectural ideology. Trained both as an artist and as a designer of theatrical stage sets, he understood well the emotive power of image. He was not concerned with what a structure's materials actually consisted of, but rather what they appeared to be. This building was constructed of brick but treated to appear as granite. The columns were wooden but painted to simulate stone. The building served primarily as a library but could quickly be modified

Fig. 24. Smith Hall, University of North Carolina, Chapel Hill, photographer and date unknown, North Carolina Collection, University of North Carolina Library at Chapel Hill.

Fig. 25. Alumni Hall, Interior. Photographer unknown, photograph ca. 1900. North Carolina Collection, University of North Carolina, Library at Chapel Hill.

to serve other, seemingly incongruous, functions: Act I, Library; Act II, Ballroom. Other large and more complex classically-inspired buildings were later constructed on the university campus (most notably works of the firm McKim, Mead and White in the early twentieth century). No other building on this famous campus, however, would so endear itself both to alumni and to the citizens of the state as Playmakers Theatre.

While Robert Donaldson provided initial introductions and continual support for Davis, it would be Governor Morehead, Donaldson's college mate in Chapel Hill, who introduced the architect to the Piedmont's progressive, newly-monied elite. Among these new industrialists was Edwin M. Holt, the future textile magnate of Alamance County and a close friend of Governor Morehead. Holt, having seen an engraving of Davis's in the January 1849 issue of the *Horticulturist* (fig. 26), wrote to Davis requesting clarifications and a design for additions to his house. He observed

> I would here remark that all the designs that I have seen are better calculated for a
> Northern than a Southern climate; you must recollect that we of the South never have

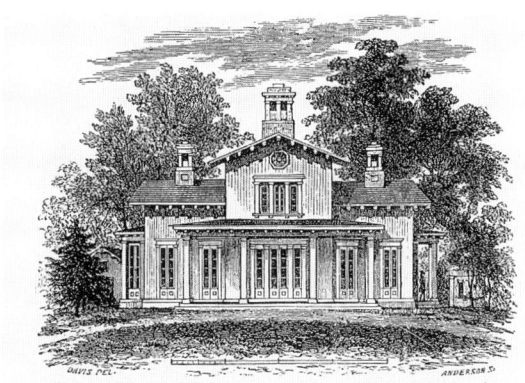

Fig. 26. Small Classical Villa, from *The Architecture of Country Houses* by A. J. Downing, published in 1850, engraving, artist unknown.

Fig. 27. Locust Grove, Alamance County, photographer unknown, 20th century photograph. North Carolina Division of Archives and History.

Fig. 28. Montrose, Hillsborough, perspectives by A. J. Davis, 1851. Courtesy of the Historic Preservation Foundation of North Carolina, Inc.

the kitchen, the wash and wood house in our dwellings, our Kitchen is always in a separate building. I would also remark that our climate requires our sleeping apartments to be more roomy & better ventilated than the North.[15]

Holt was referring to a design entitled "Small Classical Villa" which also appeared in A. J. Downing's 1850 publication *The Architecture of Country Houses*. The resulting design, executed in wood, is something of a marriage of the designs he proposed for Governor Morehead and Dr. Weir in nearby Greensboro—it has a central gable, commanding chimney stacks, oriel and bay windows and, true to most of his North Carolina residential commissions, it was basically symmetrical. Davis's design for Edwin M. Holt was liberally interpreted by local carpenter Eli Denny (fig. 27)[16].

In 1850, Davis visited Montrose, the Hillsborough home of former governor, former United States senator and Secretary of the Navy, William A. Graham, for the purpose of designing additions to the house.[17] Davis made sketches of the existing residence and submitted two plans to Graham (fig. 28). The grander plan, an Italianate villa, resembled Blandwood, while the alternate "Old English" version was reminiscent of Davis's unexecuted design for Dr. Weir.

Though his wife approved of both designs, Secretary Graham found them too grand for Hillsborough. Aspects of each plan were used in the final design, although the Italianate tower was never built. Considering Graham's social and political standing, the fully realized commission for Montrose would have been an important ornament for Davis, an architect consistently concerned with his stature. Montrose burned in 1862.[18]

In 1851 and 1853 respectively, the Female College and the Edgeworth Female Academy, both located in Greensboro, contacted Davis for plans for new educational facilities.[19] A surviving nineteenth-century photograph of the Female College's additions show long casement windows with drip mouldings—Romantic features characteristic of Davis's work. The only image of the Edgeworth Female Academy, found on the cover of sheet music, does not reveal any architectural characteristics associated with Davis's designs.

In 1852, Jesse Lindsay, John Motley Morehead's brother-in-law and a banker, state legislator, and devout Presbyterian, had his brother Robert visit Davis in New York to request additions and alterations to his home in Greensboro. Davis transformed the existing frame house into a bracketed Italianate villa (figs. 29 and 30). While this commission was not among Davis's most important, the front elevation is an early appearance of a building motif which became popular across the nation in the years following the Civil War. This design motif appeared frequently in recommendations of Davis and Downing and greatly influenced vernacular residential design in North Carolina for more than 50 years after their initial distribution. Versions of this central-gabled, bracketed house eventually appeared in every corner of the state.

Fig. 29. Jesse Lindsay House. Alexander Jackson Davis Collection, New York Historical Society.

Fig. 30. Jesse Lindsay House, photographic image courtesy of Barbara H. Church.

Overtures were also made to Davis in 1854 by the trustees of Salem College to design a new facade for Main Hall on Salem Square, located in the Moravian town of Salem. While Davis likely provided a design, the college ultimately built a monumental Doric portico designed by a local Moravian entrepreneur, Francis Fries.[20]

In 1857, John Motley Morehead also commissioned a hotel and courthouse from Davis—both to be located in Greensboro. Neither project was built and the drawings do not survive.

The architect was summoned for his last visit to Chapel Hill in July 1856. A growing student population and an expanded curriculum prompted additional space requirements. Davis sent drawings for improvements to the university in September. His designs included adding a new Italianate cornice, cupola, and portico to South Building and a dome and additions to the old chapel. With these proposed additions, together with the last in a series of Romantic masterplans, Davis fulfilled the aspirations of his friend and patron, Robert Donaldson, as requested years before: "Give them grand plans. . . . A handsome gate or two . . . a belt of trees. . . . The Hall of Doric, Ionic or Tuscan Order."[21] (fig. 7)

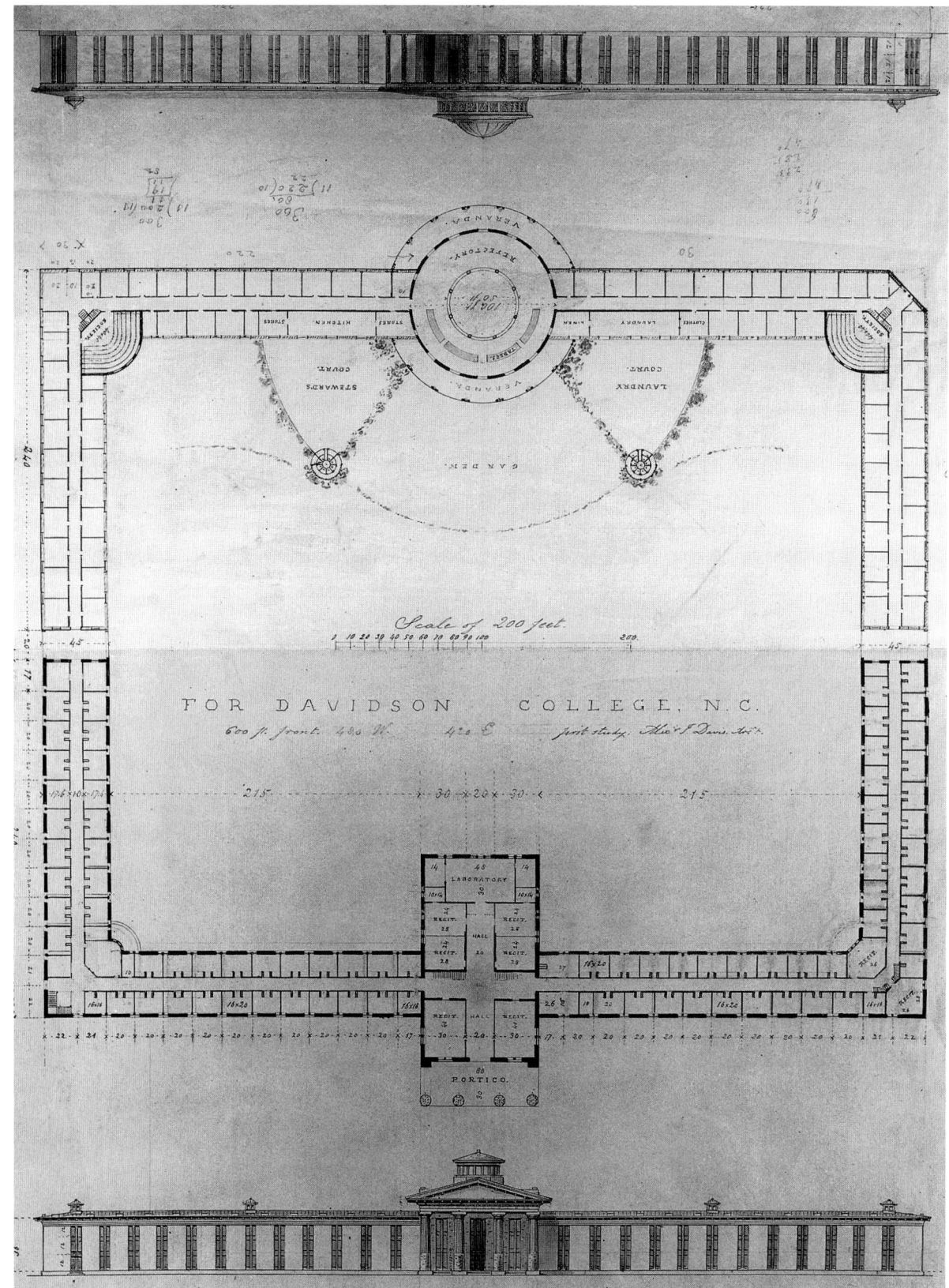

Fig. 31. Davidson College, Davidson, drawing by A. J. Davis, 1856. Metropolitan Museum of Art, Harris Brisbane Dick Fund, 24.66.435.

Hillsborough builder John Berry was invited to bid and comment on Davis's proposals for the university. He declared that the old chapel would not support a dome and the proposed enlargements.[22] Berry had never constructed a dome; this may have accounted for his reservations. The trustees, therefore, determined that the monies would be more wisely expended on new construction. Davis was contacted about these new buildings, but the commissions were ultimately awarded to William Percival. This decision was based, no doubt, upon Percival's claims that his revolutionary central heating and ventilation system would save the university maintenance fees. This "revolutionary" heating system was an immediate failure.

Davis's last major commission for the state was for Davidson College, a Presbyterian institution located in the Piedmont just west of Charlotte. It was one of his largest and most important commissions.

Maxwell Chambers, an eccentric and munificent Salisbury merchant, died in 1855. He willed the college between two and three hundred thousand dollars. Despite legal difficulties and compromises due to lawsuits from Chamber's relatives, Davidson received $234,299.00. This gift made Davidson one of the wealthiest educational institutions in the nation.

The selection of Davis as architect for the campus was an obvious one. An abbreviated list of institutions which had commissioned his services included New York University, the University of Michigan, Virginia Military Institute, and Yale University. He had also established himself as the architect for the homes and institutions of North Carolina's progressive and largely Presbyterian leadership.

While in Raleigh some years earlier, Davis met Dr. Drury Lacy, a Presbyterian minister and educator. Dr. Lacy was appointed president of Davidson College in 1854 and, at his suggestion, the college trustees contracted with Davis to design a mammoth new facility. A letter from Mrs. Lacy to her stepdaughter in August of 1856 explained the results:

Fig. 32. Davidson College, Chambers Hall. Courtesy of Davidson College.

Fig. 33. Davidson College Library, Davidson. Courtesy of Davidson College.

Your father got back from Salisbury this morning, bringing the plan of the new building, which I hav'nt had a chance to examine yet, except to see that it is one great big building.[23]

Mrs. Lacy also observed that Davis had "spruced up amazingly, having taken himself a wife."[24] The trustees had instructed Davis to provide a design for a multipurpose facility which would accommodate both student and faculty housing, and academic functions—all under one roof. With the exception of the chapel, the old campus, loosely based on Thomas Jefferson's University of Virginia, was to be demolished as the entire plan was realized.

Relying on his large institutional designs previously provided for the Pauper Lunatic Asylum in New York and for the Lunatic Hospital in Raleigh, Davis created an enormous quadrangle resembling an English college in plan. Davisean windows flanked the two central and colossal Tuscan blocks—one with a dome and semicircular colonnade and one with a gable roof, pedimented portico and circular belvedere (figs. 31 and 32).

Only one segment (80 feet by 140 feet) of the proposed complex was completed. This portion, appropriately named Chambers Hall, was one of the largest, most modern and architecturally powerful

Fig. 34. Davidson College Commencement Chapel, Davidson. Courtesy of Davidson College.

college building designs in the nation at the time. The ground floor housed three laboratories and several large classrooms. A 20-foot wide hallway cut through the center of the building and another ran perpendicular to it, connecting the dormitory wings to the central block. The upper levels housed a large library located at the front of the building and an 80-foot by 80-foot commencement chapel located at the back (figs. 33 and 34). Of the chapel, a reporter for the *North Carolina Presbyterian* commented:

> It is unquestionably the most beautiful room in the State of North Carolina. Nothing that we have seen can be compared with it. It is very large, capable of holding, we suppose, 1000 persons, and the seats have been so admirably arranged that the speaker [at] the rostrum can be easily seen by everyone.[25]

In his rendering of the Davidson College masterplan, one of Davis's most elegant drawings, he located Romantic villas of varying styles in the rolling Piedmont hills beyond the powerful Tuscan composition (fig. 1). This idealized image, more than any other of his many proposals for North Carolina, represents what he and Robert Donaldson had proposed for the rural state. The design for Davidson College was A. J. Davis's grandest academic composition. Paul Turner, in his publication on American campus planning wrote:

Nothing epitomizes the ambitious mid-nineteenth-century spirit of American college building better than this design by Davis for Davidson College. The stark neoclassical forms fortified the myth of the classical curriculum with its roots in antiquity.[25]

The Civil War ended this great era of progress, and the state's ruined economy halted all construction for governmental and educational institutions in North Carolina. With no more public or private commissions forthcoming, A. J. Davis's work in the South was finished. His career fell into decline after the war, and he received only a handful of commissions in the 1870s and 1880s, many of which were not executed.

During his reign as one of America's premier architects, Alexander Jackson Davis shaped architectural fashions as few others had done. While nationally prominent architects designed buildings in North Carolina before, during, and after A. J. Davis's period, none dictated taste and fashion as elegantly or completely as Davis. He designed buildings of national importance in North Carolina, notably the State Capitol, Smith Hall at Chapel Hill, the Hospital for the Insane, Blandwood and Davidson College, and added a refreshing and Picturesque character to the state's architectural landscape.

Edward T. Davis is an architectural historian for the State of North Carolina. He received his Bachelor of Architecture from Virginia Polytechnic Institute and State University, has studied under Peter Hodson at Portsmouth University and at The Architectural Association in England, and under Charles Brownell at The University of Virginia. He is curator of the exhibition, A Romantic Architect in Antebellum North Carolina: The Works of Alexander Jackson Davis.

---

[1] *Raleigh Register,* 23 February, 1844. In *Architects and Builders in North Carolina,* Catherine W. Bishir records in greater detail the skepticism with which out-of-state architects were met by the general public.

[2] Hugh Talmadge Lefler, *North Carolina. The History of a Southern State* (Chapel Hill: The University of North Carolina Press, 1954), 298.

[3] A.J. Davis Daybook I, 15 March, 1828, Davis Collection, New York Public Library, New York.

[4] Charles Brownell, "An Introduction to the Career of Alexander J. Davis, 1803-1892," for the exhibition, *A Romantic Architect in Antebellum North Carolina: The Works of Alexander Jackson Davis.* 1995.

[5] The building was much altered by architect Hobart Upjohn in the early twentieth century. The current antapilasters, columns, portico and spire all date from this remodeling. The windows, front doors and fanlights, and the sanctuary walls appear to date from the 1832 structure.

[6] Robert Donaldson to David Swain, 12 November, 1843, Swain Collection, Southern Historical Collection, University of North Carolina.

[7] A. J. Davis to David Swain, 24 March, 1845, Swain Collection, Southern Historical Collection, University of North Carolina.

[8] For additional information on Blandwood's role in the Italianate movement in American, see Jane Davies, "Blandwood and the Italian Villa Style in America," *Nineteenth Century,* I, (September 1975): 11-14.

[9] Ibid.

[10] A. J. Davis Daybook I, 23 January, 1844, Davis Collection, New York Public Library, New York.

[11] A.J. Downing, *Cottage Residences* (New York, NY: Wiley and Putnam, 1842), 15.

[12] Morehead to Davis, 16 December 1849, Davis Collection, New York Public Library, New York.

[13] John V. Allcott, *The Campus at Chapel Hill: Two Hundred Years of Architecture* (Chapel Hill, NC: Chapel Hill Historical Society, 1989), 36-37.

[14] Davis's November 7, 1850 entry in his diary records that the New York firm of Crane and Smith carved the four capitals for a sum of $10.00 total. Alexander Jackson Davis, Daybook, Metropolitan Museum of Art, New York.

[15] Edwin M. Holt to A. J. Davis, 2 March, 1849, Davis Collection, New York Public Library. For additional information on the Holt house, see Bishir, *North Carolina Architecture* (Chapel Hill, NC: University of North Carolina Press, 1990), 243, and Bess Beatty, "The Edwin Holt Family: Nineteenth-Century Capitalists in North Carolina," *North Carolina Historical Review,* 63, no. 4: 511-35.

[16] Bishir, *North Carolina Architecture,* 480.

[17] John V. Allcott, "Architectural Developments at Montrose in the 1850s," *North Carolina Historical Review,* 42, No. 1 (January 1965): 85-95.

[18] Ibid.

[19] Davis Diary, Metropolitan Museum of Art, 47.

[20] A. J. Davis Daybook I, 30 October, 1853. Davis Collection, Avery Architectural and Fine Arts Library, Columbia University, New York. For additional information on Fries's and Davis's roles in the design of this portico, see footnote 86, Bishir, *North Carolina Architecture,* 478.

[21] Donaldson to Davis, 16 January, 1844, Davis Collection, New York Public Library.

[22] Swain to Berry, quoted in Lane, *Architecture of the Old South: North Carolina,* 254.

[23] Mrs. Drury Lacy to her stepdaughter, 6 August, 1856. Davidson College, Davidson College Manuscripts Collection.

[24] Ibid.

[25] Mary D. Beaty, *A History of Davidson College* (Davidson: Briarpatch Press, 1988), 65.

[26] Paul Turner, *Campus: An American Planning Tradition* (Cambridge, Massachusetts, 1984), 125.

Alexander Jackson Davis and the North Carolina State Capitol

JOHN L. SANDERS

INTRODUCTION

The North Carolina State Capitol of 1840 is a major example of an American civic building in the Greek Revival style. While it is nationally known for its excellence of design, materials, and execution and for its nearly unchanged internal form and entirely original exterior appearance, it also plays an important local role as the vital center and symbol of North Carolina state government.

During the last three decades, the Capitol has undergone extensive, intermittent rehabilitation and conservation. That continuing work is intended to return the structure to and to keep it in sound physical condition, to make it fully functional as both a historic site and an office building, and to exhibit its interior architectural features and finishes and in part its furnishings as they were during its first quarter century of use (1840-65).

Among its distinctions, the Capitol was designed in large part by the New York architectural firm of Ithiel Town, Alexander Jackson Davis, and James H. Dakin, and it is the only one of their three state capitols that survived the nineteenth century. (The Connecticut Capitol at New Haven and the Indiana Capitol at Indianapolis were the other two capitols from their office.) Jane B. Davies, principal biographer of Davis, ranked the North Carolina Capitol and the Customs House in New York City, built in the same decade, as the firm's two most important civic buildings.[1]

All informed writers about the Capitol have ascribed its design at least in part to Town and Davis. (Dakin, though a member of the firm during the early phase of the Capitol's design, is rarely mentioned in that connection.) Although attempts have been made to determine the respective design contributions of the Town and Davis firm and of the other architects who preceded and followed them on the project, no prior effort to distinguish the design roles of Town and Davis as between themselves has been published.

North Carolina State Capitol, Raleigh, Senate Chamber, photograph by Tim Buchman, 2000

Fig. 35. North Carolina State House, Raleigh, engraving by Goodacre ca. 1825. Courtesy of John Sanders.

This monograph treats specifically the work of Alexander Jackson Davis in North Carolina. That purpose drives the inquiry, what contributions did Davis himself make to the design of the North Carolina State Capitol? (Davis had no direct hand in the Capitol's construction, and he did not visit the site until four years after its completion.)[2]

No confident and detailed answer to that query is possible, for several reasons.

First, many years of diligent searching have discovered not one plan or drawing of the Capitol by any hand that was in North Carolina when the structure was being planned and built, though there are contemporary references to many such documents that were sent to or created in North Carolina. (There are several relevant plans and elevations in the four collections of Davis manuscripts in New York City that are helpful to this inquiry, but none of them reached North Carolina in the 1830s.)[3]

Second, no correspondence or other writings from the 1830s have been found that record Davis's personal role in designing the Capitol, save for Davis's office records of his execution of plans and drawings that could as well have reflected Town's ideas as Davis's own. The North Carolina Commissioners for Rebuilding the Capitol dealt face-to-face and by mail with Town (who came to Raleigh three times in 1833-34 to meet with them), but they never saw Davis and may not even have known of his participation in the project. (This arrangement was common to all of the firm's state capitol design undertakings except perhaps for Connecticut.) Town presumably dealt with Davis in person on design matters, and so they would have had little occasion to write about their respective roles in the process.

Third, Davis in his later years always credited the Capitol to Town and himself jointly, sometimes including David Paton in the credits, but he did not distinguish his own role from Town's in its design.

The analyst who would differentiate the design role of Davis from that of his senior partner therefore must resort to surmises that are based largely on limited knowledge of the state of plans for the Capitol just before Town and Davis entered upon the commission, written evidence of a few changes made in those plans on Town's recommendation, drawings Davis prepared and retained in the firm's New York office files as they reflect design decisions, and general observations of contemporaries and later students of the firm about the respective strengths and working methods of the two partners.

DESIGN EVOLUTION TO 1833

Any discussion of the design evolution and the roles of the designers of the Capitol must begin with a description of its predecessor and prototype, the State House.[4] (North Carolina usage has consistently given that designation to the 1796 building and "Capitol" to the 1840 building.)

The new town of Raleigh was established in 1792 to serve as the centrally located, permanent capital of the state. On Union Square, near its center, the designer-carpenter Rhodam Atkins built between 1792 and 1796 a plain, two-story, hip-roofed, brick, late Georgian State House to accommodate the General Assembly, the courts, and the state executive officers other than the Governor, whose office was at his residence. From the centers of the long eastern and western fronts projected pedimented entrance pavilions, quotations from Tryon Palace in New Bern that were ordered by the General Assembly to give the drab design a lifting touch of grace.

By 1819, the State House needed repairs and enlargement. William Nichols, an English-born and -trained builder and architect who had practiced in North Carolina for nearly 15 years, was engaged as state architect. Nichols enlarged the State House and largely rebuilt its interior between 1820 and 1824. A third floor was added. The central eastern and western pavilions were extended to form short wings, which were fronted with rusticated basements carrying pseudo-porticoes, each with four heroic, engaged Ionic columns supporting a pediment. That feature gave the structure a cruciform plan and a neoclassical cast. The exterior was stuccoed and probably was scored to suggest stone. A domed rotunda was constructed at its center to house Antonio Canova's marble statue of George Washington, earlier commissioned by the state. In the remodeled State House, Nichols combined the architectural features that henceforth would characterize American state capitols: central portico(es) on the long dimension(s) and an external dome expressing a central rotunda, flanked by balanced wings housing the two legislative chambers—only the second such structure to do so (fig. 35).[5]

The State House was accidentally burned on 21 June 1831. Canova's *Washington* was severely damaged by the fire, though various charlatans assured state officials that it could be restored.

The legislature of 1832-33 established and elected the Commissioners for Rebuilding the Capitol and gave that five-member body full authority to contract for the design and construction of a new Capitol. In the authorizing legislation, the General Assembly directed that:

> [T]he general plan of the said Capitol shall be the same as the former building, with such an extension of length and height, as may be deemed necessary for the better accommodation of the General Assembly, the lower story of which at least shall be built of stone, and the roof covered with zinc, or other fire proof material.[6]

The General Assembly appropriated $50,000 to begin the work and gave the Commissioners charge of the state-owned quarry near Raleigh.[7]

The Commissioners had before them the largest construction task undertaken in North Carolina to that time; yet it was an assignment with definite and limited dimensions.

First, the Capitol had to accommodate all of state government—legislative, executive, and judicial.

Second, it was then thought that Canova's statue of Washington could be restored from its fragments, and a suitable place for its display had to be provided in the Capitol.

Third, the Commissioners and their architects were, from the beginning, quite determined to build a Capitol that would be an object of state pride and national admiration.

Unable to obtain a satisfactory bid on the whole job of constructing the Capitol, the Commissioners decided to be their own general contractor. They hired a building superintendent and had the site cleared. They determined to build the structure entirely from stone—gneiss, a metamorphic form of granite—from the nearby state quarry.[8]

Apparently no style other than the neoclassical was considered by the Commissioners. The refurbished North Carolina State House had been an early exhibit of that style as applied to civic buildings. They also had the familiar national precedents of Jefferson's Capitol of Virginia and the Capitol of the United States, both Roman in inspiration. By 1833, however, Greece had largely superseded Rome as the source of the architectural vocabulary for both public and private buildings that made pretensions of stylishness.

For the reasons stated earlier—lack of drawings and other helpful documentation—tracing the formal actions of the Commissioners in developing a design must rely on secondary sources.

At their second meeting, late in February of 1833, the Commissioners for Rebuilding were reported to have

> engaged in examining the various plans that they have been submitted. . . . No plan in detail has yet been fixed upon, it being conceived important that this point should remain undetermined as long as may be, so that the progress of the building is not thereby retarded, in order that as much information as possible may be collected in relation to the most appropriate models and styles of architecture for such buildings.[9]

We do not know the sources of all of those "various plans" that were before the Commissioners early in 1833. No design competition was held. William Nichols, who had enlarged and improved the State House a decade earlier, probably offered his ideas. One sure source of plans was the New York firm

Fig. 36. Alabama State Capitol, Tuscaloosa, Alabama, photographer unknown, photograph ca. 1900. Courtesy of John Sanders.

of Town, Davis, and Dakin. Ithiel Town (1784-1844) and Alexander Jackson Davis (1803-1892) had formed Town and Davis 1 February 1829; James H. Dakin (1806-1852) became a partner 1 May 1832 and withdrew 1 November 1833.[10] Town began his career as a carpenter and contractor and became an architect through study and practice. He was the businessman and promoter of the firm. One of the leading exponents of the Greek Revival style, he had recently (1827) designed the Capitol of Connecticut at New Haven in the form of a Greek Doric temple. The younger Davis was a superb delineator or "architectural composer," a designer without practical building experience.[11]

Town was well connected in North Carolina. He had built one of his patented wooden lattice truss bridges over the Cape Fear River at Fayetteville in 1819-1823, living there during part of that period, and retained a major shareholder's interest in the Clarendon Bridge Company that operated it as a toll bridge.[12] This activity brought Town acquaintance with several of the leading men of the state.[13] These contacts Town refreshed through at least annual bridge-related business visits to North Carolina throughout the 1820s and 1830s. Thus, Town understandably showed early and confident interest in designing the new Capitol for North Carolina.

In the fall of 1831, scarcely four months after the State House had burned, Town and Davis's office records show that they were working on a "Design for a State Capitol, N. Carolina."[14] November and December 1831 entries in Davis's business records indicate further work on the North Carolina project, the latter entry reading:

Drawing plan. N.C. State house. also plan for city hall/model of Parthenon.[15]

Town was in North Carolina in June 1832 on bridge business, and characteristically would have used that opportunity to pursue his interest in the commission for the Capitol's design.[16] Late in 1832, Davis noted in his business journal "Design Perspective State House, N.C."[17]

DESIGN EVOLUTION, 1833 TO 1835

Under date of 9 February 1833, just as the Commissioners for Rebuilding were setting about the task of planning the Capitol, appears in Town, Davis, and Dakin's office accounts the following intriguing entry by Davis (who was then working in the firm's Washington office):

State Capitol. North Carolina. Small perspective view for
Mr. Gaston, with plans   15 00
Large perspective view, with plans, & duplicates   100 00
Longitudinal Section, and duplicates   50 00[18]

William Gaston—sometime state legislator and congressman and Town's North Carolina lawyer—had no official role in the design or building of the Capitol.[19] Yet is obvious that he had much to do with

Fig. 37. Perspective of the proposed North Carolina State Capitol, Raleigh. Ink and wash drawing by A. J. Davis, 1832–33. A. J. Davis Collection, Metropolitan Museum of Art, Harris Brisbane Dick Fund, vol. II, p. 28.

the ultimate selection of the architects for that building. Gaston's son-in-law, Robert Donaldson of New York, was a client of the Town and Davis firm and became a particular friend of Davis.[20] It is through a letter from Susan Gaston Donaldson, Judge Gaston's daughter, that we get an early indication of the appearance of the Capitol as then contemplated by Town, Davis, and Dakin. Mrs. Donaldson wrote from New York to her father on 9 January 1833,

> I am very glad they have determined to rebuild the capitol at Raleigh—Built after the Parthenon & graced with the statue [of Washington] restored to its pristine beauty, 'twill be a monument of taste & excellence.[21]

On 24 February 1833, Gaston wrote from Raleigh to his daughter in reply:

> Say to Mr. Donaldson that the Commissioners . . . have before them Mr. Town's plans, and are well disposed I think to adopt whichever Mr. T. shall recommend. . . . I presume . . . that both Mr. D[onaldson] and Mr. T. are in favor of that which is without dome, surrounded by columns, and understood to be upon the exact model of the Parthenon. So supposing I pressed upon the Commissioners to adopt it.[22]

From Gaston's letter, it appears that Town, Davis, and Dakin then had at least two plans before the Commissioners, both of them for temple-form buildings, one with a dome (like Indiana) and the other without (like New Haven). These probably were the plans Davis had drawn earlier in February.

That the firm should have submitted a temple-form plan is not surprising. Town's Connecticut Capitol, the first to put a Greek Doric temple to that use, was scarcely two years old and had drawn much acclaim. In their winning 1831 design for the Indiana Capitol, as in their successful 1833 design for the Customs House in New York, they had perched a dome atop a Doric temple. Four of the firm's temple-form designs for the North Carolina Capitol have been found. Two of them are small, finished floor plans of a building with hexastyle (six-columned) porticoes at each end and bold antae along its flanks.[23]

The perspective drawing illustrated in fig. 37, although it does not carry any legend, has often been identified as a representation of the Connecticut Capitol at New Haven.[24] In fact, it is the firm's proposed design for the North Carolina Capitol, without dome. The ten antae along the flanks and the six columns and steps of the end porticoes match those features in one of the detailed 1833 floor plans that is labelled by the artist, "Design for the State-House, N.C." (The New Haven capitol had no antae along its flanks.) A version of this perspective drawing probably was considered by the Commissioners for Rebuilding when they rejected the temple-form design early in 1833.

A second perspective drawing (actually a pencil tracing by Davis of his original drawing), illustrated in fig. 38, appears to be of the domed version of a capitol for Raleigh.[25] The tracing bears no identification, but it corresponds in external features to one of the North Carolina Capitol floor plans noted above, it dates stylistically from the 1832-33 period, and it is not a representation of any other known Davis building. Thus the original of this drawing (or another very similar one) was reviewed by the Commissioners early in 1833.

Fig. 38. Perspective of the North Carolina State Capitol, Raleigh. Graphite tracing by A. J. Davis of Davis drawing, 1832–33. A. J. Davis Collection, Metropolitan Museum of Art, Harris Brisbane Dick Fund, 24.1966.1407 (58).

The Commissioners for Rebuilding, however—contrary to Gaston's speculation—were not interested in a Greek temple for North Carolina, so Town, Davis, and Dakin were unsuccessful in their effort to erect one of their civic temples, with or without dome, in Raleigh.

The Commissioners considered themselves bound by the specification of the 1832-33 General Assembly in the rebuilding act that "the general plan of the said Capitol shall be the same as the former building. . . ."[26]

That plan of "the former building" had been the creation of William Nichols in his State House improvements of 1820 to 1824. He had then gone to Alabama and designed and built at Tuscaloosa between 1827 and 1831 a State Capitol that was a grander version of his North Carolina State House. (That building is gone but good photographs of it exist [fig. 36])[27]

Apparently Nichols, who was then practicing in Alabama, acting with and through his son, William Nichols, Jr., who was in Raleigh, presented to the North Carolina Commissioners early in 1833 a plan for an improved version of the Alabama Capitol, to be built entirely of stone, and the Commissioners accepted it, at least as a general scheme.[28] While the Commissioners dealt in person only with the younger Nichols, it is probable that the primary design work was done by the elder Nichols. The younger Nichols left no record of other architectural work, and the Commissioners looked to both of them as responsible parties in this instance.

At their meeting on 2 April 1833, the Commissioners were reported by the *Raleigh Register* to have

determined on the size and plan of the Building, and the manner in which the Work shall be executed. In conformity with the Act of the Assembly, . . . they have decided that the Building shall be three stories high, 160 feet long, 64 feet wide, with East and West Wings, 40 feet front, projecting 30 feet. The basement [first] story will accommodate the Public Officers; the second story the Legislature and its Clerks, and the Supreme Court, and furnish a capacious Room for the State Library; and the third story will contain Rooms for the Engrossing Clerks, &c.

> The dimensions of the Capitol being fixed upon, Mr. Wm. Nichols, Jun. is engaged to prepare the Plan of the Building and to make out the proper specifications. . . . If any further architectural skill be found necessary, Mr. Nichols, or his father, on being requested to do so, will pay occasional visits to Raleigh during the progress of the Work.[29]

William Nichols, Jr., laid a draft plan before the Commissioners on 20 May 1833. On 4 June, Nichols suggested and the Commissioners approved small adjustments in the dimensions of the ground plan and the addition of angle pavilions at each end of the east and west fronts.[30] On 26 July 1833, Nichols was paid for the whole of his professional services to the State $350, a sum that suggests a substantial amount of work.[31] And that was the end of the personal connection of the Nicholses, father and son, with the planning and construction of the North Carolina State Capitol. There is no direct evidence of difficulty or dissatisfaction with them; they simply disappeared.

The surviving state records report no face-to-face dealings by Town with the Commissioners prior to August of 1833, though the evidence earlier noted reveals the firm's active interest in the commission from late 1831 and pursuit of it from early 1833, if not earlier. From April through July of 1833, it appeared that Town, Davis, and Dakin had been entirely shut out by the Nicholses.

Yet on 14 August 1833, less than three weeks after William Nichols, Jr., had completed his work and been paid, Ithiel Town was in Raleigh recommending to the Commissioners changes in the Nichols plan.[32] It is likely that William Gaston was the agent of the firm's recovery. Perhaps the Commissioners realized that the grand edifice their ambition demanded could not be realized from the limited Nichols plan they had approved.

On Town's recommendation, the Commissioners made several changes in the approved Nichols design, with the general effect of making it more decidedly Greek in aspect. Square heads were substituted for arched heads of the exterior ground floor doors and windows, for example, and the intended rustication of the ground-floor walls was eliminated except for the east and west wings. The most significant change made upon Town's urging was the addition of the fully developed tetrastyle (four-columned) Greek Doric porticoes on the east and west fronts, replacing pseudo-porticoes of engaged columns, probably intended to have been in Nichols's favored Ionic order, which he used on the Raleigh State House and the Tuscaloosa and Jackson, Mississippi capitols.[33]

Clearly, Town was now in control and was busily transforming the Nichols plan into an unmistakable product of his own firm. Town's changes were not more extensive because the foundation had already been laid to the height of three feet by the time he began to advise the Commissioners in August of 1833. Though bound to the cruciform Nichols plan and its basic program, the Town firm so fully made the design their own that some writers have assumed it to be entirely of their creation.[34]

Early in November of 1833, Davis entered in his office records the following note of work done:

View of N.C. State house, with plan, for Mr. Town to present to Mr. Gaston	10.00
View smaller of same with single plan of principal floor.	Ditto
View for my small book.[35]	

A Romantic Architect in Antebellum North Carolina: The Works of Alexander Jackson Davis

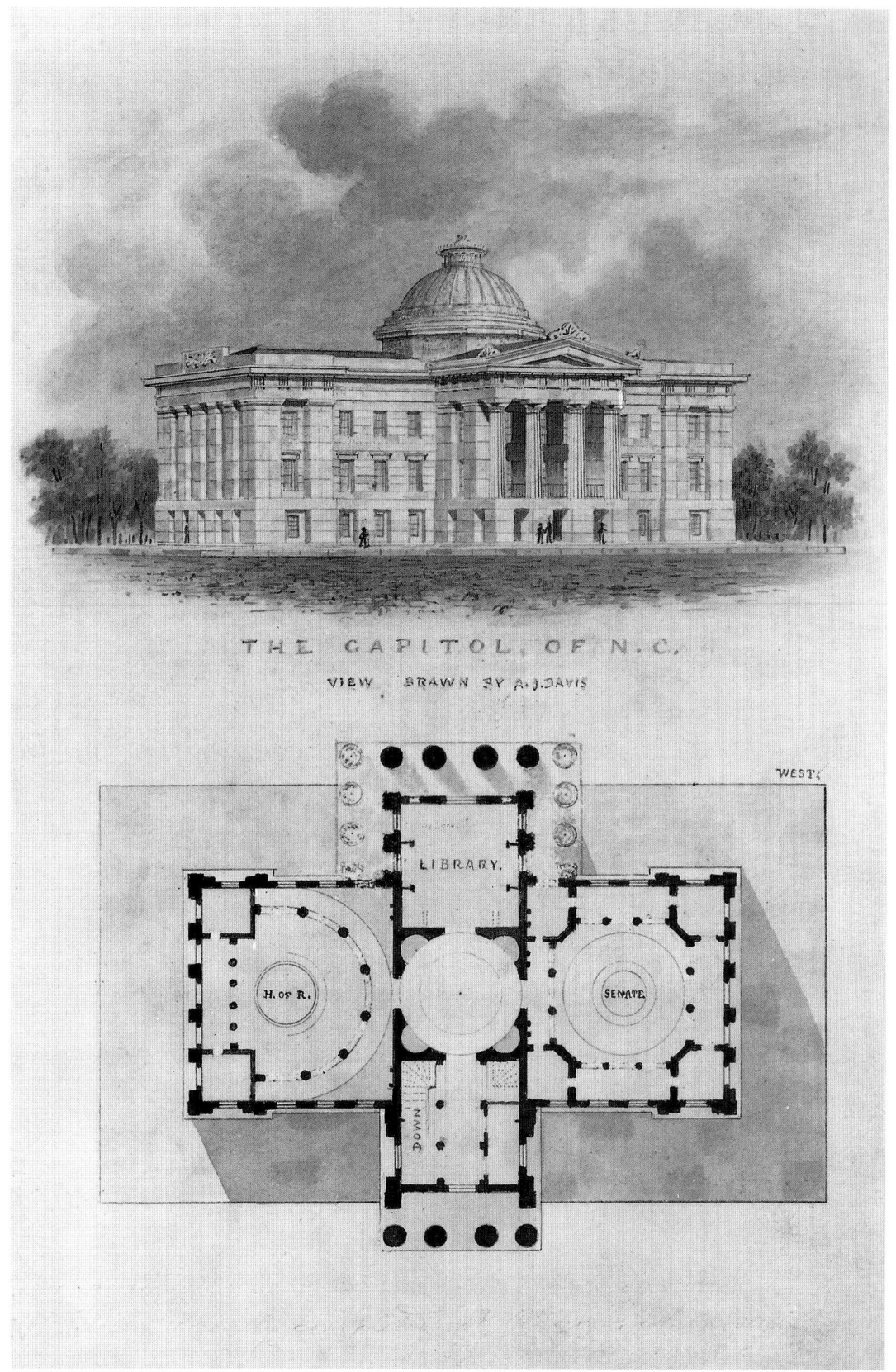

Fig. 39. Perspective and Plan of the North Carolina State Capitol, Raleigh, drawing by A. J. Davis, ca. 1833. Metropolitan Museum of Art, Harris Brisbane Dick Fund, 24.66.140(23).

The "View smaller" probably was the ink and watercolor perspective view of the Capitol (fig. 39), the only known view of the exterior of the cruciform Capitol by Davis that dates from the 1830s. This perspective exhibits the fully matured transformation of the Nichols-devised cruciform plan into Town and Davis's own work (Dakin had left the partnership by that date). Note particularly the row of bold antae or deep pilasters along the south (left) flank, a hallmark of the firm whose earlier invention Jane B. Davies has attributed to A. J. Davis.

Town was again in Raleigh on 4 January 1834, when he received $250 for his services to date.[36] Further drawings for the Capitol were prepared by the firm in May and June of 1834. The surviving documents and drawings sketchily reflect the evolution of the plan for the Capitol between August of 1833, when Town, Davis, and Dakin became the Commissioners' architects, and late 1834, when the Commissioners considered the plan to be well settled.

There are only four known Davis drawings of the cruciform Capitol that date from 1833 to 1835, in addition to the perspective view noted earlier. One drawing from 1833-34 shows the intended plans of the first and second floors,[37] the second (from mid-1834) is a plan of the second (legislative) floor only,[38] the third is a longitudinal (north-south) section (fig. 40)[39] and is a near companion to the second drawing, and the fourth is a cross section of the rotunda.[40] The general disposition of functions on the second floor (legislative chambers, Supreme Court Chamber, and State Library Room) corresponds to that of the Nichols scheme; how closely the forms of the legislative chambers resemble those intended by the superseded Nichols plan it is not possible to know.

While the design of the Capitol developed, the work of construction went on remarkably unaffected by the lack of a definitive plan. William S. Drummond of Washington was hired as superintendent on 12 January 1833, the site was cleared, the state quarry was opened, and a horse-powered railroad was built to move stone from the quarry to the construction site. On 4 July 1833, the cornerstone was laid.[41]

By mid-1834, dismissals and resignations among the top-level managers of the project left the Commissioners in need of a general supervisor. At their request, Ithiel Town in New York sent down David Paton (1801-1882), an Edinburgh-born and -trained architect who had worked briefly for Sir John Soane in London, to be clerk of the works.[42] Paton later maintained that, at the same time he entered into the contract with the State on Town's initiative, he contracted privately with Town to undertake

> The preparation of the designs and drawings to be required during the progress of the work; for which he was to be remunerated by Mr. Town himself out of his professional allowances from the Commissioners.[43]

After a visit to Raleigh in October of 1834, Town wrote to Davis, praising progress of their Capitol and Paton's management.[44] By the beginning of the year 1835, Paton had sufficiently gained the favor of the Commissioners that he was able to persuade them to make changes in the agreed-upon Town and Davis plans. The principal change, one that enraged Town, was the substitution of a more traditional timber truss system in place of Town's intended lattice truss system to support the roof above the legislative chambers. One effect of that change was to require a greater vertical rise for the roof framing system,

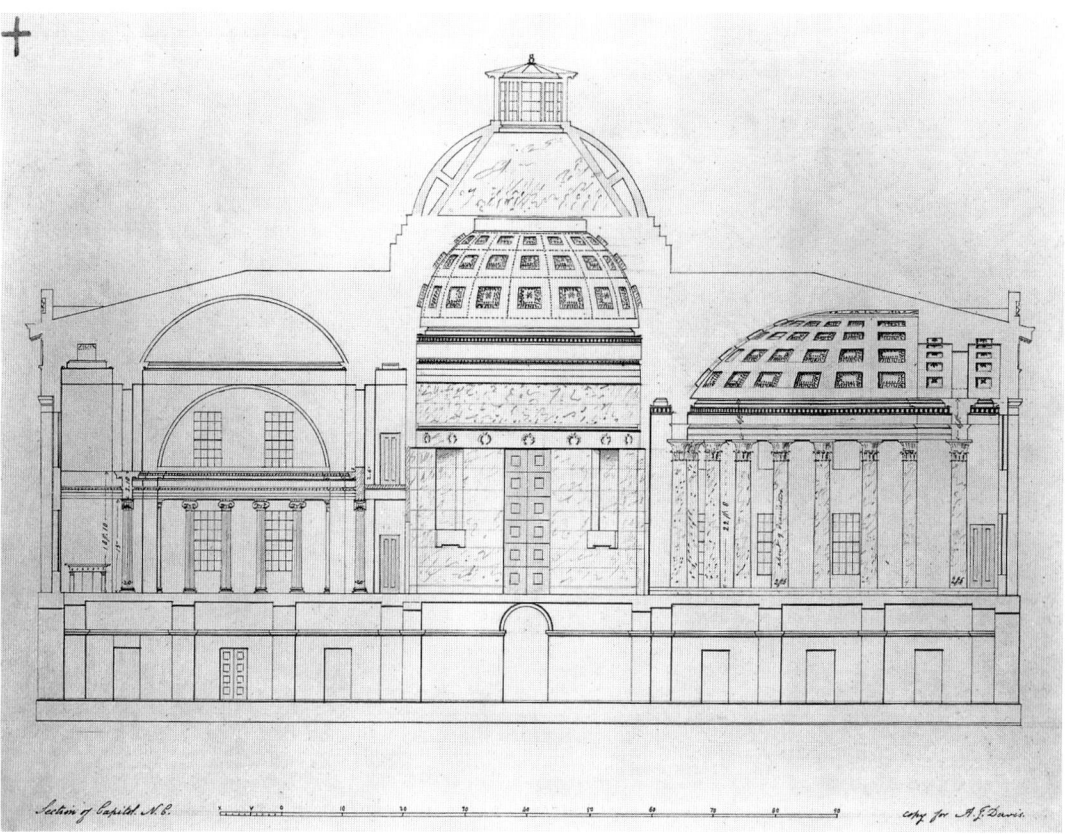

Fig. 40. North Carolina State Capitol, Longitudinal Section, Raleigh, drawing by A. J. Davis, 1834. Metropolitan Museum of Art, Harris Brisbane Dick Fund, 24.66.759.

resulting in lower ceiling heights in the legislative chambers and a higher and bolder exterior roof line (compare figs. 40 and 41). Town threatened to have Paton dismissed, but apparently he found Paton so strongly supported by the Commissioners that his only recourse was to withdraw quietly from the project.[45]

As a result, by mid-1835, Paton was designated by the Commissioners as their "sole Architect and Director, as well as Superintendent and Inspector," to use his self-description.[46] Apparently the Commissioners, finding that Paton was doing nearly all of the architectural work, decided to economize by discontinuing the relationship with Town. For the Capitol commission, Town and Davis received a total of $550 in professional fees.[47]

Construction, 1834-1840

Although the basic design of the Capitol was well established and the exterior walls were forty feet high when Paton arrived in Raleigh in September 1834,[48] he was able to make a number of changes. He vaulted the first-floor offices and corridors in masonry as a fireproofing measure. He moved the Supreme Court Chamber and the State Library Room from their intended locations on the second floor to the third, thus providing space in the east and west wings of the second floor for legislative committee rooms off the stair halls and more commodious accommodations above for the court and the library. He designed the top-lit, third-floor vestibules to the library and court rooms (fig. 42), added public

Fig. 41. North Carolina State Capitol, Longitudinal Section, Raleigh, drawing by William Tate Daggett, School of Design, North Carolina State University, 1925.

galleries in the legislative chambers at the third-floor level, and introduced the circular opening in the second floor of the rotunda (fig. 43). He supervised the construction of the upper portions of the exterior walls, the porticoes, the drum and dome, and all of the interior of the Capitol. Therefore, though he was working largely to the designs of others, he fully earned the praise of Talbot Hamlin for "the beautiful execution which guaranteed the effectiveness of the building."[49]

Regrettably, the good relations that had subsisted between Paton and the Commissioners soured near the end of the project and in the spring of 1840, just before its completion and dedication, he was dismissed.[50] The cause seems to have been Paton's insistent pleas for higher compensation on the ground that he had provided considerably more extensive professional services than were required by his original contract with the State (the result of duties he initially performed under private contract with Town) without adequate recompense by the State.

THE ROLE OF DAVIS

Returning to the theme of this chapter, what was the role of Alexander Jackson Davis in designing the Capitol?

As noted earlier, in his numerous lists of his own architectural works, made later in life, Davis always wrote that the Capitol was jointly designed by himself and Town, without distinguishing their respective roles; sometimes he also treated David Paton as a participant in the design.[51]

William Dunlap's 1834 publication, *A History of the Rise and Progress of the Arts of Design in the United States,* in an entry based on information provided by Davis, stated that Davis was "the joint architect with Mr. Town . . . [of] the capitol of North Carolina. . . ."[52]

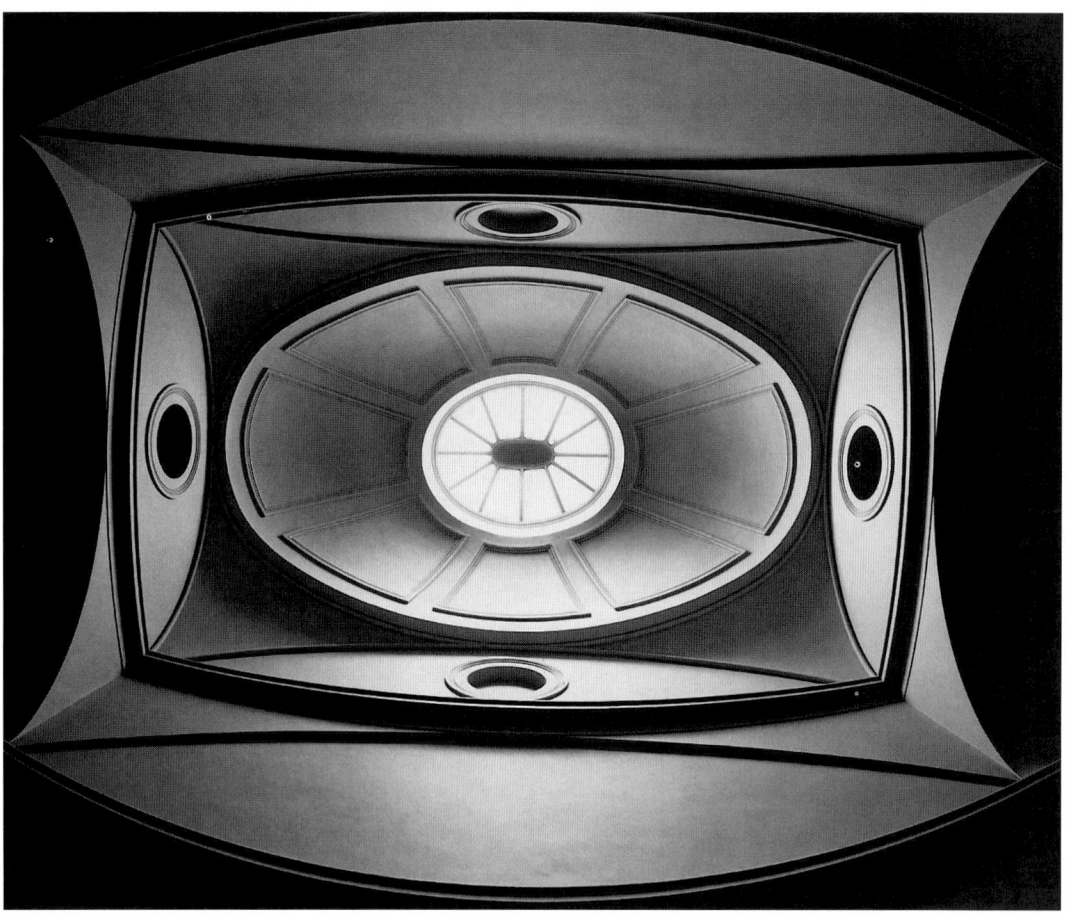

Fig. 42. North Carolina State Capitol, Raleigh, Third-Story Passage Dome, photograph by Tim Buchman, from *North Carolina Architecture* by Catherine W. Bishir, 1990.

What was the usual working relationship between the two partners?

James Gallier, Sr., (1798-1866) wrote in his *Autobiography* (1864), that in 1832 "[t]here was, . . . properly speaking, only one architect's office in New York, kept by Town and Davis. Town had been an carpenter, but was no draftsman. . . . Davis, his partner, was no mechanic, but a good draftsman, and possessed much taste as an artist. . . ."[53]

Davis himself wrote that "Town was possessed with invention and a proper feeling for the beauties of moral classical art."[54] Several of Town's buildings that antedated his connection with Davis, including the Gothic Trinity Church and the Greek Doric Capitol, both built on the Green in New Haven, and several residential commissions as well, testify to Town's skill as a designer, despite his lack of facility at the drafting table.[55] Town was capable of contributing fully to design decisions respecting works on which he joined forces with Davis or with other architects.

Talbot Hamlin, in his magisterial *Greek Revival Architecture in America*, wrote that, in determining the relative contributions of Town and his various collaborators on joint architectural projects,

> it would be foolish to under estimate the importance of Town's influence and personality. . . . Town was evidently a man of powerful personality, a great job getter, but also a

scholar and an idealist. . . . Just how important he was as a designer it is almost impossible to discover. Certainly both with [Martin] Thompson and with his more famous partner, Alexander Jackson Davis, the greater amount of the actual drafting and detailed study of the problems was left to his partners. It is probably also true that the design was chiefly theirs too.[56]

Jane B. Davies, the closest recent student of the Town and Davis firm, has written:

Unique in New York in its day, the office had the finest architectural library in America, and it united the diverse talents of men intent on professional careers: the experienced, practical Town; the imaginative, innovative Davis; and the able, enterprising young Dakin. Town was unquestionably the head of the firm. His prestige, ability, and contacts brought many of the commissions. Although frequently away from the firm for several weeks or months, he was usually there for the designing of important works. He shared the design process with his partners; some designs were worked out jointly, while others were done independently during his absences. Credit for design authorship is often difficult to determine, but Davis's records and drawings contain numerous indications, and responsibility can also be deduced from the partners' whereabouts.[57]

The surviving finished drawings from the 1830s with respect to the Capitol appear to be the work of Davis, and all or nearly all of the firm's office record entries relating to those drawings appear to credit them to him. None of these drawings can be identified as Town's work.

No working drawing for the Capitol from the firm's office has been found; in fact, such drawings may never have been prepared by the firm. As earlier noted, Paton wrote that he contracted directly with Town, separate from his engagement with the State to serve as clerk of the works, to prepare architectural drawings of the kind the firm would have been expected to provide. Therefore, such detailed working drawings were done by Paton in Raleigh; certainly all of them were his work after early 1835, when he officially superseded the New York firm as the Capitol architect. He took away with him at least 229 Capitol-related drawings that he had prepared, and doubtless many others were used up on the job.

A reasonable surmise, then, is that Town and Davis (but perhaps not Dakin, as Davis did not credit him with participation) agreed, at least in general terms, on revisions to be made in the Nichols plan the Commissioners for Rebuilding had approved in July of 1833, and that the preparation of the various presentation drawings and other visual representations of the agreed-upon scheme was left to Davis. If Town was available to review Davis's drawings before they were sent to Raleigh, he probably did so. Given Davis's universally lauded skills as a pictorial designer and illustrator, his contributions to the proportions, harmony, coherence, and finish of the composition doubtless were major. His presentation drawings typically were superb in composition and execution — so much so that one overlooks the absence of such mundane essentials as fireplaces and chimney stacks. Perhaps even Town was at times swept along in the torrent of Davis's artistic eloquence, as were so many of their firm's clients.

And what did this mean for the design of the Capitol?

Fig. 43. North Carolina State Capitol, Raleigh, Rotunda, photograph by Tim Buchman, from *North Carolina Architecture* by Catherine W. Bishir, 1990.

The Capitol surely has a purer Greek character than it would have had from the hand of the Nicholses, if we may judge from William Nichols's constructed capitols in Raleigh, Tuscaloosa, and Jackson. Both the fully developed east and west porticoes and the bold pilastrades across the north and south fronts are Town and Davis's contributions. The House of Representatives Chamber of the United States Capitol, the work of Benjamin Henry Latrobe and Charles Bulfinch, clearly was the model for the House Chamber in the Capitol. Davis was intimately familiar with the Washington prototype, having then recently drawn floor plans and views of the United States Capitol, including the House Chamber.[58] Both of the legislative chambers of the Capitol, whose designs followed the Davis plans except for the reduced ceiling heights and smaller number of columns in their surrounding screens of columns, are more functional as well as better proportioned and detailed than were those of William Nichols in his Raleigh, Tuscaloosa, and Jackson capitols.

The harmonious composition, architectural authenticity, and purity of line of the North Carolina State Capitol owe a great deal to the skill of Alexander Jackson Davis in design and exposition. Without his contributions, it is unlikely that the architectural historian Wayne Andrews would have characterized this as "the most distinguished of all our state capitols. . . ."[59]

John L. Sanders is a Professor of Public Law and Government Emeritus of the Institute of Government at The University of North Carolina at Chapel Hill. He received his A.B. and J.D. from UNC-CH and has done extensive research on the design and construction of the North Carolina State Capitol. He is widely recognized as the leading expert on the Capitol and has published several articles on the building.

---

[1] Jane B. Davies, "Introduction: Alexander J. Davis, Creative American Architect," in *Alexander Jackson Davis, American Architect, 1803-1892,* ed. Amelia Peck (New York: The Metropolitan Museum of Art and Rizzolli, 1992), 21.

[2] Alexander Jackson Davis, Day Book, 1827-53, entry for 30-31 Jan. 1844, reproduced in John V. Allcott, *The Campus at Chapel Hill: Two Hundred Years of Architecture* (Chapel Hill: The Chapel Hill Historical Society, 1986), 29.

[3] The principal collections of Davis drawings and manuscripts are in the Print Department of The Metropolitan Museum of Art, New York; the Avery Architectural and Fine Arts Library of Columbia University in the City of New York; the Manuscript Division of the New York Public Library; and the New-York Historical Society, New York.

[4] For the general history of the design and construction of the State House (1792-1831) and Capitol (1833-present), see John L. Sanders, "The North Carolina State Capitol of 1840," *The Magazine Antiques* 128 (September 1985): 474-84, and "This Political Temple, the Capitol of North Carolina," *Popular Government* 43, No. 2 (Fall 1977): 1-10; Catherine W. Bisher, *North Carolina Architecture* (Chapel Hill and London: University of North Carolina Press, 1990), 163-72; and Catherine W. Bisher, Charlotte V. Brown, Carl R. Lounsbury, and Ernest H. Wood III, *Architects and Builders in North Carolina: A History of the Practice of Building* (Chapel Hill and London: University of North Carolina Press, 1990), 163-67.

[5] Stephen Hill's Pennsylvania State Capitol at Harrisburg (built, 1817-1822) was the first of the type. Henry-Russell Hitchcock and William Seale, *Temples of Democracy: The State Capitols of the USA* (New York and London: Harcourt Brace Jovanovich, 1976), 63.

[6] N.C. Laws 1832-33 chap. 3.

[7] *Ibid.*

[8] "The New Capitol," *Raleigh Register,* 18 January 1833; *Report [of] Commissioners Appointed to Superintend the Re-building of the State Capitol, December 4th, 1834* (Raleigh: Philo White, Printer to the State, 1834), 5.

[9] "State Capitol," *[Raleigh] Star,* 1 March 1833.

[10] Davies, "Davis," in *Alexander Jackson Davis,* 18.

[11] Jane B. Davies, "Town, Ithiel," in *Macmillan Encyclopedia of Architects,* ed. Adolf K. Placzek (New York: Free Press, 1982), IV, 220-23; — "Davis, Alexander Jackson," *ibid.,* I, 505-14;—, "Town and Davis," *ibid.,* IV, 223-24; Roger Hale Newton, *Town & Davis, Architects: Pioneers in American Revivalist Architecture, 1812-1870, Including a Glimpse of Their Times and Their Contemporaries* (New York: Columbia University Press, 1942), 95-108; Talbot Hamlin, *Greek Revival Architecture in America: Being an Account of Important Trends in American Architecture and American Life Prior to the War Between the States* (New York, London, and Toronto: Oxford University Press, 1944), 137-40.

[12] Richard Sanders Allen, *Covered Bridges of the South* (Brattleboro, Vermont: The Stephen Green Press, 1970), 4; Newton, *Town & Davis, Architects,* 43-44, 73.

[13] For instance, William Gaston was Town's attorney. See William Gaston to Ithiel Town, Raleigh, 5 July 1822, ALS in Miscellaneous Collections: William Gaston, Manuscript Division, New York Public Library.

[14] Alexander Jackson Davis, Day Book, 1827-53, MS, 492. In A. J. Davis Collection, Manuscript Division, New York Public Library, under designation of "Diary."

[15] Davis, Day Book, 1827-53, MS, 125.

[16] Davis, Day Book, 1827-53, MS, 117,133.

[17] Davis, Day Book, 1827-53, MS, 143.

[18] Alexander Jackson Davis, Journal, 1827-91, MS, 39. In A. J. Davis Collection, Print Department, Metropolitan Museum of Art, New York.

[19] Charles H. Bowman, Jr., "Gaston, William Joseph," in *Dictionary of North Carolina Biography,* ed. William S. Powell (Chapel Hill: The University of North Carolina Press, 1986), II, 283-85; John L. Sanders, *William Gaston as a Public Man* (Chapel Hill: North Caroliniana Society, Inc., and North Carolina Collection, 1997), 1-16.

[20] J. V. Allcott, "Donaldson, Robert, Jr.," *Dictionary of North Carolina Biography,* 1986, II, 92.

[21] Susan Gaston Donaldson to William Gaston, 9 January 1833, ALS in William Gaston Papers, Southern Historical Collection, Wilson Library, The University of North Carolina at Chapel Hill.

[22] William Gaston to Susan Gaston Donaldson, 24 February 1833, ALS in William Gaston Papers, Southern Historical Collection.

[23] Design for State House, N.C., MS drawings 45-4 and 45-5 in A. J. Davis Collection II, Avery Library, Columbia University.

[24] Untitled ink and wash drawing in A. J. Davis Collection, vol. II, p. 28, Harris Brisbane Dick Fund, Metropolitan Museum of Art, New York.

[25] Graphite tracing in A. J. Davis Collection, no. 24.1966.1407(58), Harris Brisbane Dick Fund, Metropolitan Museum of Art, New York.

[26] N.C. Laws 1832-33 chap. 3.

[27] C. Ford Peatross, *William Nichols, Architect* ([Tuscaloosa:] The University of Alabama Art Gallery, 1979), illustrations 18 and 19, p. 40.

[28] "The New Capitol," *Raleigh Register,* 9 April 1833.

[29] *Ibid.*

[30] *Report [of] The Joint Select Committee to Whom was Referred the Report of the Commissioners Appointed to Rebuild the Capitol, December 23d, 1834* (Raleigh: Philo White, Printer to the State, 1834), 3.

[31] *Report [of] Commissioners Appointed to Superintend the Re-building of the State Capitol, December 4th, 1834* , 5.

[32] *Report [of] The Joint Select Committee to Whom was Referred the Report of the Commissioners Appointed to Rebuild the Capitol, December 23d, 1834,* 3.

[33] *Ibid.,* 3-4.

[34] Newton, *Town & Davis, Architects,* 160-61.

[35] Davis, Day Book, 1827-53, MS, 156.

[36] Receipt signed by Ithiel Town, Raleigh, 4 January 1834, MS in State Treasurer's Papers, State Archives, Division of Archives and History, Department of Cultural Resources, Raleigh.

[37] Plan for Capitol of N.C. at Raleigh, ink and wash drawing in A. J. Davis Collection, Harris Brisbane Dick Fund, Metropolitan Museum of Art, New York.

[38] Plan of Principal Floor, Capitol, N.C., ink and wash drawing in A. J. Davis Collection, Harris Brisbane Dick Fund, Metropolitan Museum of Art, New York.

[39] Architectural drawing: Section of Capitol, N.C., ink drawing in A. J. Davis Collection, Harris Brisbane Dick Fund, Metropolitan Museum of Art, New York.

[40] Plan and elevation rotunda, Capitol, Raleigh, N.C., ink and wash drawing in A. J. Davis Collection, Harris Brisbane Dick Fund, Metropolitan Museum of Art, New York.

[41] "The New Capitol," *Raleigh Register,* 9 April 1833; *Raleigh Register,* 16 July 1833.

[42] Contract between Ithiel Town for the Commissioners for Rebuilding the Capitol and David Paton, 10 September 1834, MS in David Paton papers, P.C. 644, State Archives, Raleigh; John L. Sanders, "Paton, David," *Dictionary of North Carolina Biography,* 1994, V, 29-30.

[43] Memorial of David Paton . . . To His Excellency John M. Morehead Governor of the State of North Carolina, 26 October 1842, MS in Legislative Papers, Box 595, Session of 1842-43, State Archives, Raleigh.

[44] Ithiel Town to A. J. Davis, Ohio River (near Portsmouth), 24 October 1834, ALS in A. J. Davis Collection, Print Department, Metropolitan Museum of Art, New York.

[45] Ithiel Town to David Paton, New York, March 1835 (postmarked Washington, 31 March 1835), ALS in Disbursement of Public Buildings, 1833-1836, State Treasurer's Papers, State Archives, Raleigh.

[46] Memorial of David Paton, 1842.

Fig. 44. North Carolina State Capitol, Raleigh, photograph by Tim Buchman, 1990.

⁴⁷ *Report [of] Commissioners Appointed to Superintend The Re-building of the State Capitol, December 4th, 1834,* 5.

⁴⁸ *Report [of] The Joint Select Committee to Whom was Referred the Report of the Commissioners Appointed to Rebuild the Capitol, December 23d, 1834,* 4.

⁴⁹ Hamlin, *Greek Revival Architecture in America,* 197.

⁵⁰ Memorial of David Paton, 1842.

⁵¹ For example, in a manuscript list entitled "Works of A. J. Davis," written by Davis late in his life, he recorded: "1833. Capitol of N.C. at Raleigh. Designed in concert with I. Town[.] Superintended by Paton, a studied Architect[,] English." MS in Scrapbook, vol. II, leaf 9, A. J. Davis Collection, Print Department, Metropolitan Museum of Art, New York.

⁵² William Dunlap, *A History of the Rise and Progress of the Arts of Design in the United States* (1834: reprint, New York: Dover Publications, Inc., 1969), II, 410-11.

⁵³ As quoted in Hamlin, *Greek Revival Architecture in America,* 141.

⁵⁴ Newton, *Town & Davis, Architects,* 60.

⁵⁵ Hitchcock and Seale, *Temples of Democracy: The State Capitols of the USA,* 83.

⁵⁶ Hamlin, *Greek Revival Architecture in America,* 137, 138; see also 175-176.

⁵⁷ Davies, "Town and Davis," in *Macmillan Encyclopedia of Architects,* IV, 223-24.

⁵⁸ A. J. Davis, illustrations 168-178 and 180-180.5, in Pamela Scott, *Temple of Liberty: Building the Capitol for a New Nation* (New York: Oxford University Press, 1995); Newton, *Town & Davis, Architects,* 168.

⁵⁹ Wayne Andrews, *Architecture in America: A Photographic History From the Colonial Period to the Present* (New York: Atheneum Publishers, 1977), 42.

A Romantic Architect in Antebellum North Carolina: The Works of Alexander Jackson Davis

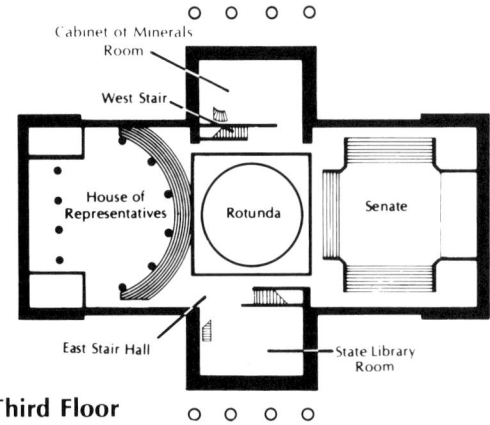

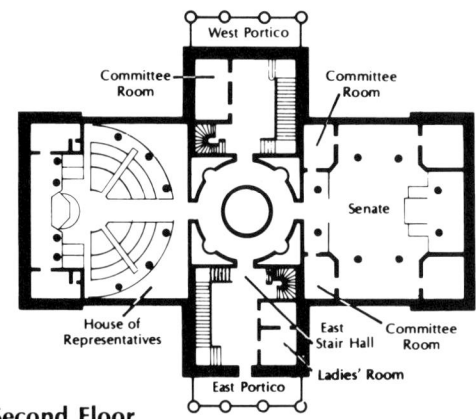

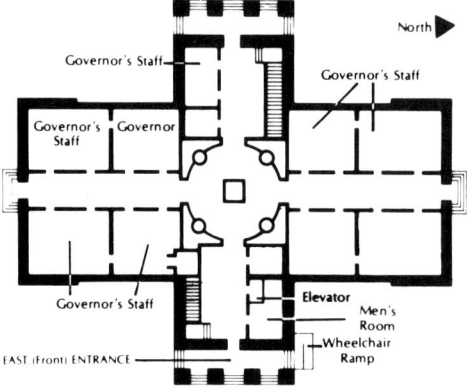

Fig. 45. State Capitol. Floor plan with current uses of space.

The Works by Alexander Jackson Davis in North Carolina
Compiled by Edward T. Davis

This list contains Davis's known works, both executed and unexecuted, as recorded in his records. The author is deeply indebted to the late Jane B. Davies for her chronology of Davis's "Works and Projects" in *Alexander Jackson Davis, American Architect 1803-1892*, as well as to the pioneering writings of the late John V. Allcott of the University of North Carolina at Chapel Hill.

1831
First Presbyterian Church, Fayetteville. Town and Davis. The only surviving image of this structure was drawn by a child in the late nineteenth century; therefore it is not known to what extent the builders followed Town and Davis's design. Town's patented lattice truss roof-framing system survives. Extant, though greatly altered.

1832
Philanthropic Society Building, University of North Carolina, Chapel Hill. Town and Davis. Tuscan Revival. Not executed.

1833-1840
North Carolina State Capitol, Raleigh. William Nichols, Jr., Town and Davis, David Paton. Greek Revival. Extant.

1834
Roman Catholic Church for Judge William Gaston, New Bern. Gothic Revival. Not executed.

1835
Monument to Joseph Caldwell, former president of the University of North Carolina. Intended for the campus of the University of North Carolina. Obelisk on Neoclassical pedestal. Not executed.

1844-1845
Additions to East and West Buildings, University of North Carolina, Chapel Hill. Bracketed Style. Extant.

1844-1856
Designs for alterations to South Building (Greek Revival), the Chapel (Neoclassical), and a campanile (Tuscan Revival), and several masterplans. The South Building alterations and the Chapel and campanile designs were not executed. Portions of the masterplan were executed.

1844
Blandwood, extensive additions to the house of Governor John Motley Morehead, Greensboro. Italianate. Extant.

1844
House for Dr. David Weir, Greensboro. Gothic Revival. Not executed.

1845
Presbyterian Church, Chapel Hill. Tuscan Revival. Destroyed by fire in 1919.

1849-1852
Alumni (or Smith) Hall, University of North Carolina, Chapel Hill (now known as Playmakers Theatre). Greek Revival. Exterior extant. Interior altered.

1849
Locust Grove, House for Edwin M. Holt, Alamance County. Tuscan Revival. Extant.

1850-1852
North Carolina Hospital for the Insane, Raleigh. Tuscan and Roman Revival. A portion of this building, much altered, is extant.

1850
Alterations and additions to Montrose, house for the Secretary of the Navy, William A. Graham, Hillsborough. Davis offered both Gothic Revival and Tuscan Revival alternatives. Neither was built as Davis had proposed, however Hillsborough builder John Berry incorporated aspects of the Tuscan Revival design in the realized building. The house was destroyed by fire in 1862.

1851
Additions to the Female College, Greensboro. Greek Revival. Destroyed by fire circa 1905.

1852
Alterations and additions to a house for Jesse Lindsay, Greensboro. Tuscan Revival. Destroyed.

1853
Alterations and additions to Edgeworth Female Academy, Greensboro. The only surviving image of this building, found on the cover of late nineteenth-century sheet music, does not suggest that the Academy followed Davis's designs.

1853
Portico for Main Hall, Salem College, Salem. Greek Revival. Francis Fries, acting on behalf of the Academy, contacted Davis in 1853 concerning a new Greek Revival portico for the Main Hall of Salem Academy. The resulting portico is strongly reminiscent of Davis's work, but the only surviving drawing of the portico is signed by Fries. Extant.

1856-1860
Davidson College Campus, Davidson. Tuscan Revival. Only a portion of this vast complex was realized. Chambers Hall, as this building was named, burned in 1924.

1856
Infirmary, University of North Carolina, Chapel Hill. Neoclassical. The only recordation of this modest structure, a late nineteenth-century photograph housed in the North Carolina Collection at the University of North Carolina at Chapel Hill, reveals a modest one-story frame building with Neoclassical detailing. The building was destroyed circa 1900.

Bibliography

Allcott, John V. "Architect A.J. Davis in North Carolina." *North Carolina Architect 20* (1973): 10-15.

_____. "Architectural Developments at Montrose in the 1850's." *North Carolina Architect 42* (1965): 85-95.

_____. "Donaldson, Robert, Jr." In *Dictionary of North Carolina Biography*, ed. William S. Powell. Chapel Hill and London: University of North Carolina Press, 1986. Vol. II.

_____. "Robert Donaldson, the First North Carolinian to Become Prominent in the Arts." *North Carolina Historical Review 52* (1975): 333-64.

_____. "Scholarly Books and Frolicksome Blades: A.J. Davis Designs a Library-Ballroom." *Journal of the Society of Architectural Historians 33,* 1974.

_____. *The Campus at Chapel Hill: Two Hundred Years of Architecture.* Chapel Hill: The Chapel Hill Historical Society, 1986.

Allen, Richard Sanders. *Covered Bridges of the South.* Brattleboro, Vermont: Stephen Green Press, 1970.

Anderson, Jean Bradley. *Carolinian on the Hudson: The Life of Robert Donaldson.* Raleigh: The Historic Preservation Foundation of North Carolina, Inc., 1996.

Andrews, Wayne. *Architecture in America: A Photographic History from the Colonial Period to the Present.* New York: Atheneum Publishers, 1960.

Battle, Kemp. *History of the University of North Carolina.* Raleigh: Edwards and Broughton, 1907, 1912.

Beaty, Mary D. *A History of Davidson College.* Davidson: Briarpatch Press, 1988.

Bishir, Catherine W., Charlotte V. Brown, Carl R. Lounsbury, and Ernest H. Wood III. *Architects and Builders in North Carolina: A History of the Practice of Building.* Chapel Hill: University of North Carolina Press, 1990.

Bishir, Catherine W., with photographs by Tim Buchman. *North Carolina Architecture.* Chapel Hill: University of North Carolina Press, 1990.

Bowman, Charles H., Jr. "Gaston, William Joseph." In *Dictionary of North Carolina Biography*, ed. William S. Powell. Chapel Hill and London: University of North Carolina Press, 1986. Vol. II.

Brownell, Charles E. "The Italianate Villa and the Search for an American Style, 1840-1860." In *The Italian Presence in American Art, 1760-1860."* ed. Irma B. Jaffe. New York: Fordham University Press, 1989.

_____, Richard Guy Wilson, William M.S. Rasmussen and Calder Loth. *The Making of Virginia Architecture, 17th to 20th Centuries.* Richmond: Virginia Museum of Fine Arts, 1992.

Davies, Jane B. "Blandwood and the Italian Villa Style." *Nineteenth Century I, No. 3.* New York, September, 1975.

North Carolina State Capitol, Raleigh, House Chamber, photograph by Tim Buchman, 2000

_____. "Davis, Alexander Jackson." In *Macmillan Encyclopedia of Architects,* ed. Adolf K. Placzek. New York: Free Press, 1982. Vol. I.

_____. Introduction to reprint edition of A.J. Davis's *Rural Residences.* New York, 1980.

_____. "Introduction: Alexander J. Davis, Creative American Architect." In *Alexander Jackson Davis, American Architect, 1803-1892,* ed. Amelia Peck, 8-21. New York: Metropolitan Museum of Art and Rizzoli, 1992.

_____. "Town and Davis." In *Macmillan Encyclopedia of Architects,* ed. Adolf K. Placzek. New York: Free Press, 1982. Vol. IV.

_____. "Town, Ithiel." In *Macmillan Encyclopedia of Architects,* ed. Adolf K. Placzek. New York: Free Press, 1982. Vol. IV.

_____. "Works and Projects." In *Alexander Jackson Davis, American Architect,* ed. Amelia Peck. New York, 1992.

Davis, Alexander Jackson. Letters and diaries of Alexander Jackson Davis.

Alexander Jackson Davis Collection. Avery Architectural and Fine Arts Library, Columbia University in the City of New York, Division of Drawings and Archives. New York, New York.

_____. Alexander Jackson. Alexander Jackson Davis Collection. Metropolitan Museum of Art, Print Room. New York, New York.

_____. Alexander Jackson Davis Collection. New-York Historical Society.

_____. Alexander Jackson. Alexander Jackson Davis Papers. New York Public Library, Rare Books and Manuscript Division. New York, New York.

Donoghhue, John. *Alexander Jackson Davis: Romantic Architect, 1803-1892.* Ph.D. dissertation, New York University, 1982.

Downing, Andrew Jackson. *The Architecture of Country Houses.* New York: D. Appleton, 1850.

_____. *Cottage Residences.* New York: Wiley and Putnam, 1842.

_____. *A Treatise on the Theory and Practice of Landscape Gardening Adapted to North America.* New York: Wiley and Putnam, 1841.

Dunlap, William. *A History of the Rise and Progress of the Arts of Design in the United States.* 1834; reprinted, New York: Dover Publications, Inc., 1969. 2 vols.

Graham, William A. *The Papers of William A. Graham.* ed. Max R. Williams. North Carolina Department of Archives and History, Raleigh, 1957.

Hamlin, Talbot. *Greek Revival Architecture in America: Being an Account of Important Trends in American Architecture and American Life Prior to the War Between the States.* New York, London, and Toronto: Oxford University Press, 1944.

Henderson, Archibald. *The Campus of the First State University.* Chapel Hill: University of North Carolina Press, 1949.

Hitchcock, Henry-Russell and William Seale. *Temples of Democracy: The State Capitols of the USA.* New York and London: Harcourt Brace Jovanovich, 1976.

Lane, Mills. *Architecture of the Old South: North Carolina.* New York: Beehive Press, 1985.

Lefler, Hugh, and Albert Newsome. *North Carolina: The History of a Southern State.* 3rd. ed. Chapel Hill: University of North Carolina Press, 1973.

Newton, Roger Hale. *Town & Davis, Architects: Pioneers in American Revivalist Architecture, 1812-1870, Including a Glimpse of Their Times and Their Contemporaries.* New York: Columbia University Press, 1942.

O'Brien, Raymond J. *American Sublime: Landscape and Scenery of the Lower Hudson Valley.* New York, 1981.

Owen, Scott. "Romanticism and the Picturesque" for the exhibition *A Romantic Architect in Antebellum North Carolina: The Works of Alexander Jackson Davis,* 1995.

Peatross, C. Ford. *William Nichols, Architect.* [Tuscaloosa:] University of Alabama Art Gallery, 1979.

Peck, Amelia, ed. *Alexander Jackson Davis, American Architect.* New York: Metropolitan Museum of Art and Rizzoli, 1992.

Report [of] the Commissioners Appointed to Superintend the Re-building of the State Capitol, December 4th, 1834. Raleigh: Philo White, Printer to the State, 1834.

Report [of] the Joint Select Committee to Whom was Referred the Report of the Commissioners Appointed to Rebuild the Capitol, December 23d, 1834. Raleigh: Philo White, Printer to the State, 1834.

Sanders, John L. "This Political Temple, the Capitol of North Carolina." *Popular Government* vol. 42, no. 2 (Fall 1977): 1-10.

_____. "The North Carolina State Capitol of 1840." *The Magazine Antiques* 128 (Sept. 1985): 474-484.

_____. "Nichols, William." In *Dictionary of North Carolina Biography,* ed. William S. Powell. Chapel Hill and London: University of North Carolina Press, 1991. IV.

_____. "Paton, David." In *Dictionary of North Carolina Biography,* ed. William S. Powell. Chapel Hill and London, 1991. Vol. V.

_____. *William Gaston as a Public Man.* Chapel Hill: North Caroliniana Society, Inc., and North Carolina Collection, 1997.

Schauinger, J. Herman. *William Gaston, Carolinian.* Milwaukee: Bruce Publishing Co., 1949.

Scott, Pamela. *Temple of Liberty: Building the Capitol for a New Nation.* New York and Oxford: Oxford University Press, 1995.

Swain, David L. David L. Swain Papers, Southern Historical Collection, Wilson Library, The University of North Carolina at Chapel Hill.

Tatum, George B. *Andrew Jackson Downing, Arbiter of American Taste, 1815-1852.* Ann Arbor: University of Michigan Press, 1950.

Acknowledgments

Interest in the architecture of Alexander Jackson Davis has been growing since the Metropolitan Museum's exhibition, *Alexander Jackson Davis, American Architect 1803 - 1892,* debuted in 1992. While this was the first exhibit and catalogue on this seminal American architect, the exhibit focused primarily on his northern commissions.

In 1994, Myrick Howard of Preservation North Carolina, Catherine Bishir, of the North Carolina State Historic Preservation Office, and others, concluded that the significant body of Davis's work in North Carolina deserved recognition. It was further determined that this recognition should take form as both an exhibit, designed to travel throughout the state and beyond, and a publication, which would offer greater detail to interested historians. Davis's works in North Carolina are extensive and the task of compiling a complete chronology, together with the background of this most progressive period in the state's history, was a challenging opportunity. And with any such endeavor, this was the joint effort from a number of persons and institutions to whom I am grateful.

I particularly appreciate Scott Owen and Charles Brownell's scholarly essays for the exhibition and originally intended for this manuscript. The contribution from John Sanders has greatly assisted in making this endeavor of national importance. I am grateful for his scholarship.

Thanks go to Mr. Dan Kany of the Avery Library at Columbia University for his able assistance. Thanks are due to the Metropolitan Museum of Art and the New York Public Library for lending transparencies of Davis's drawings from their collection. Many other persons have contributed to this work by agreeing to edit the manuscripts. I am particularly thankful to Jean Bradley Anderson, Catherine Bishir, Charlotte V. Brown, and Claudia Brown.

The staff of the Gallery of Art & Design at North Carolina State University is thanked for their many contributions as well as Jonathan Noffke, former Director of the Bellamy Mansion for his enthusiasm and creativity. Thanks are also due to Michael Southern, John Acker and Raymond Beck for the drawings and transparencies which they contributed for the exhibition and this publication. The exhibition's success is, in no small measure, due to the energy and drive of Beverly Ayscue, Exhibitions Coordinator for Preservation North Carolina. I am also grateful to my fellow architectural historians at the North Carolina Department of Transportation for their constant encouragement, particularly to Nancy Van Dolsen, Vanessa Patrick and Barbara H. Church.

Several important projects undertaken by Preservation North Carolina over the last several years have been possible through the generosity of Mr. Richard H. Jenrette. This exhibition and volume should be added to that impressive list.

No architectural historian who undertakes any work on Alexander Jackson Davis should fail to acknowledge their debt to Jane B. Davies, who devoted her life's work to researching and writing on this fascinating architect. Despite her illness, Ms. Davies made frequent trips to both the Metropolitan Museum and to Avery Library at Columbia University to confirm our suspicions that the perspective drawing (Figure 33) previously attributed as the Connecticut State Capitol was drawn as the Capitol at

Raleigh. Ms. Davies was my friend and ally and I will miss her.

I am thankful for the patience of my family, particularly my children Taylor and Sarah Charlotte. Their own bedtime stories have certainly suffered as I compiled this story. I would like to dedicate my own efforts to the late Sarah H. Bollinger, who had so anticipated this publication.

Preservation North Carolina and the authors of this volume are indebted to the scholarship of John V. Allcott. Mr. Allcott's pioneering research on the works of Alexander Jackson Davis was largely the foundation upon which we based our investigations.

Edward Taylor Davis
2000

The Historic Preservation Foundation of North Carolina, Inc.
Board of Directors

Sylvia C. Nash, President, Tarboro
Carl J. Stewart, Jr., Vice President, Gastonia
Virginia G. Culpepper, Secretary, Edenton
Richard E. Hunter, Jr., Treasurer, Warrenton
Benjamin F. Speller, Jr., Chairman, Board of Advisors, Durham
E. Newsom Williams, Jr., Immediate Past President, New Bern
Marion S. Covington, Honorary President, Greensboro

Lillian B. Boney, Wilmington
Phillip C. Broughton, Asheville
Sally B. Cone, Greensboro
Jeffrey J. Crow, Raleigh
Gwendolyn P. Davis, Raleigh
Samuel Bobbitt Dixon, Edenton
Ada M. Fisher, Salisbury
John H. Haley, Wilmington
R. Darrell Hancock, Salisbury
Samuel W. Johnson, Rocky Mount
Langdon E. Oppermann, Winston-Salem
William S. Powell, Chapel Hill
Steven D. Schuster, Raleigh
Katherine G. Stern, Greensboro
Virginia A. Stevens, Blowing Rock
Elizabeth L. Wright, Wilmington

Directors Emeriti
James A. Gray, Winston-Salem
Thomas A. Gray, Winston-Salem
Frances J. Moody, Chapel Hill
Robert E. Stipe, Chapel Hill
John E. Tyler II, Roxobel

The State Capitol Foundation, Inc.
Board of Directors

Rufus L. Edmisten, President, Raleigh
Barbara Boney, Vice President, Raleigh
Katie Cashion, Secretary, Greensboro
George Breece, Treasurer, Fayetteville
Caroline Stirling, Member-at-Large, Raleigh
W. W. Yeargin, Member-at-Large, Four Oaks
Brenda Pollard, SCS Chair, Durham

Jane Barbot, Raleigh
Don Beason, Raleigh
Jonathan Brookshire, Raleigh
Thomas N. Clark, Chapel Hill
Betty Ginn, Raleigh
John R. Jordan, Jr., Raleigh
Lou Mitchell, Raleigh
Charles Montgomery, Cary
Thomas Morrow, Raleigh
C. W. Sanders, Raleigh
John L. Sanders, Chapel Hill
Samuel P. Townsend, Raleigh
Gerald P. Traub, Raleigh
Joyce White, Raleigh
Jo Ann Williford, Raleigh
Jan Woodard, Raleigh

Ex-Officio Members
Senate President Pro-Tem
    Marc Basnight, Manteo
Speaker of the House
    James Black, Matthews
Dr. Jeffrey J. Crow, Raleigh
Carol C. Henderson, Raleigh